Language Teacher Research in Europe

Edited by Simon Borg

Language Teacher Research Series

Thomas S. C. Farrell, Series Editor

TESOL Teachers of English to Speakers of Other Languages, Inc.

Typeset in Sabon and Adelon
by Capitol Communication Systems, Inc., Crofton, Maryland USA
Printed by United Graphics, Inc., Mattoon, Illinois USA
Indexed by Coughlin Indexing, Annapolis, Maryland USA

Teachers of English to Speakers of Other Languages, Inc.
700 South Washington Street, Suite 200
Alexandria, Virginia 22314 USA
Tel. 703-836-0774 • Fax 703-836-6447 • E-mail info@tesol.org • http://www.tesol.org/

Publishing Manager: Carol Edwards
Copy Editor: Terrey Hatcher Quindlen
Additional Reader: Sarah Duffy
Cover Design: Tomiko Chapman

ISBN 9781931185370
Library of Congress Control Number: 2006909502

Table of Contents

Acknowledgments

Many thanks go to the contributors to this volume for their willingness to share their research. The support of TESOL in publishing this work is also greatly appreciated. The particular contributions of Thomas S. C. Farrell, Carol Edwards, and Terrey Hatcher Quindlen in bringing this project to completion are warmly acknowledged.

Series Editor's Preface

The Language Teacher Research Series highlights the role language teachers at all levels play as generators of knowledge concerning all aspects of language teaching around the world. This idea may seem alien to many language teachers. Often, they either think that they have nothing to say about their teaching or that what they have to say is of little significance. Teachers generally are accustomed to receiving knowledge from so-called *real* researchers.

In my opinion, language teachers have plenty to say that is valuable for colleagues around the world. One of the main reasons for the Language Teacher Research Series is to celebrate what is being achieved in English language classrooms each day, so we can encourage and develop communities of like-minded language teaching professionals who are willing to share these important experiences.

In this manner, the TESOL community can extend its understanding of English language teaching in local, regional, and international settings. The series attempts to cover as many of these contexts as possible, with volumes covering the Americas, Asia, Europe, the Middle East, and New Zealand/Australia. Each account of research presented in the Language Teacher Research Series is unique in the profession. These studies document how individual language teachers at all levels of practice systematically reflect on their *own* practice (rather than on other teachers' practices).

When practicing language teachers share these experiences with teachers in other contexts, they can compare and contrast what is happening in different classrooms around the world. The ultimate aim of this series is to encourage an inquiry stance toward language teaching. Teachers can play a crucial role in taking responsibility for their own professional development as generators and receivers of knowledge about what it means to teach English language learning.

How This Series Can Be Used

The Language Teacher Research Series is suitable for preservice and in-service teacher education programs. The examples of teacher research written by practitioners at all levels of teaching and all levels of experience offer a window into the different worlds of English language teachers. In this series we have attempted to impose some order by providing authors with a template of headings for presenting their research. This format is designed so that language teachers with varied expertise and educational qualifications can pick up a book from any region and make comparisons about issues, background literature, procedures taken, results, and reflections without having to work too hard to find them. The details in each chapter will help readers compare and evaluate the examples of teacher research and even replicate some research, if so desired.

This Volume

This volume in the Language Teacher Research series, *Language Teacher Research in Europe*, documents different forms of practitioner inquiry that involve systematic, intentional, and self-critical inquiry about language teaching in different European settings. It will be interesting for the reader to compare and contrast these research stories from Europe with studies from *Language Teacher Research in Asia*, the first volume published in this series, as well as from the other volumes in the series.

Thomas S. C. Farrell, Brock University, Canada

CHAPTER 1

Language Teacher Research in Europe

Simon Borg

Teacher research refers to "all forms of practitioner enquiry that involve systematic, intentional, and self-critical inquiry about one's work" (Cochran-Smith & Lytle, 1999, p. 22). It goes beyond thoughtful teaching of the kind often associated with reflective practice and should also involve, as Freeman (1998) argued, making public one's findings. This notion has a long history in the field of education (e.g., Stenhouse, 1975), and more recently a number of book-length guides for teachers on the subject (Campbell, McNamara, & Gilroy, 2004; Lankshear & Knobel, 2004) have demonstrated the continuing interest in it. The emergence in recent years of evidence-based practice (EBP) as a model for professional action in education has emphasised even further the idea that teachers' engagement in research is desirable. A fundamental argument behind EBP is that when teachers are able to engage in research and to make justified pedagogical decisions informed by sound research evidence, this will have a beneficial effect on teaching and learning (Davies, 1999). Although the precise manner in which this research should or can take place has been the subject of much debate, it is generally accepted that more teacher involvement in research can enhance the quality of education.

In the field of TESOL, although varied perspectives have been adopted in defining what teacher research is and how it relates to the process of teaching (Burns, 1999; Freeman, 1998), a similar overall message emerges: enquiring into their own practices, individually or collectively, is a process which benefits teachers' professional growth and pedagogical activity.

Although the value of teacher research is widely discussed in the field of English language teaching, evidence of teacher research is less conspicuous. One of the reasons this volume is valuable, then, is that it makes available to a wide readership concrete examples of teacher research conducted by language teaching professionals. These professionals work in a range of different language teaching contexts, yet the contributions to this volume are united by the way in which they adhere to the definition of teacher research presented here: they all illustrate and make public ways in which professionals in the field have systematically examined, in their own working contexts, issues of immediate relevance to them and their learners. Collectively, the research reported in this volume highlights the many methodological forms which teacher research can assume and the manner in which it can be applied to a diverse range of professional issues, problems, and challenges. The chapters in this volume are also united in the way that they highlight several characteristics shared by teacher researchers: a desire to grow professionally, a determination to improve the quality of education that learners experience, a commitment to innovation and constant self-evaluation, and an interest in sharing their work with others.

Whilst acknowledging these positive aspects of teacher research, however, the authors do not pretend that their research was accomplished without problems. On the contrary, the contributors candidly describe the different types of challenges they encountered in their research. Ultimately, however, by focusing on the benefits of enquiring into teachers' own professional practices, this collection makes a persuasive argument for the relevance and value of teacher research to our field generally.

Language Teacher Research in Europe presents research conducted by language teachers at different levels, from high school English teachers to English language teacher educators. The countries represented cover a range of European contexts stretching from England to Turkey. In terms of the volume's organization, the chapters are presented in alphabetical order of the first author's surname and each chapter follows the same pattern of main headings: Issue, Background Literature, Procedures, Results, and Reflection. This common structure supports the coherence of the collection and facilitates the reader's ability to make comparisons across the chapters.

The first study, presented in the chapter "Primary School EFL Teachers as Researchers," examines the experience of language teachers who are learning to be researchers. Working with a group of primary school teachers in Turkey, Derin Atay documented the process she went through in facilitating a professional development course designed to support these teachers in conducting research in their own classrooms. Drawing on field notes and journals, this study highlights the successes of the course in motivating teachers to do research. It also, however, provides clear evidence of the obstacles, particularly heavy work-loads and a lack of time, which may deter teachers from engaging in research. There are clear implications in this study for the conditions required if teachers are to perceive teacher research as a feasible undertaking.

The next chapter, "Teaching Web-Mediated EAP to Ethnic Minority Students," evaluates the design and implementation of an English for academic purposes (EAP) programme devised for ethnic minority undergraduates at a British university. Mihye Harker and Dimitra Koutsantoni used formative data, summative data, and follow-up telephone interviews with participants to assess the extent to which the course fulfilled its key objective of supporting the development of students' academic writing skills in English. Overall, the data suggest that the programme was successful. Students responded positively to the content and organisation of the EAP materials and to the Web-based approach used to deliver them. The authors also note that end-of-course tests revealed improvements in students' academic writing compared to diagnostic tests taken at the start. Further, interviews indicated that students felt the course might have longer-term benefits for their academic studies. In addition to these positive outcomes, the data highlight areas in which the course could be improved.

In a chapter from Hungary, "Are You Doing Well in English? A Study of Secondary School Students' Self-Perceptions," Judit Heitzmann explores secondary school learners' thoughts and feelings about their own successes and failures in learning a foreign language. Drawing on interviews, written narratives, and self-assessment data from learners, the study illustrates how teachers can find out what learners feel about their own learning. In this case, learners indicated positive attitudes towards studying English, and they recognised their responsibility for working to learn effectively. The study also highlights interesting differences in the way Hungarian learners defined success in language learning compared to British learners.

A chapter from Spain, "The Integration of Literature: A Way to Engage Learners' Intellect and Interest," provides an account of Sacramento Jáimez-Muñoz's experiences in designing and implementing an English course based on literature. Drawing on the notion of literature with a small *l*, she collected data during one academic year through questionnaires, observations, her own reflections, and test scores. She analysed these data to compare the experiences of two classes of secondary school learners. One group participated in the new literature-based course the author designed, and the other group used the prescribed textbook. Whilst acknowledging the challenges involved in designing and implementing the new programme, Jáimez-Muñoz finds evidence of improved learning, enhanced autonomy, and greater motivation in the experimental group.

"Teachers Into Researchers: Learning to Research in TESOL" is the second chapter in this volume which focuses on the processes of learning to do research. In this case, Richard Kiely examines the experiences of students on an MA programme at a British university. After describing the novel approach to teaching research methods adopted on this programme, Kiely reports how he examined questionnaires, interviews, and students' written and oral work (including their final dissertations) to assess the impact the course had. Overall, the data suggest that students felt the course helped them develop as researchers, not just in terms of their practical skills but also by allowing them to develop a researcher identity. This study, together with those by Derin Atay and Anna Franca Plastina, will be of particular interest to readers whose work involves teaching research methods.

In the chapter titled "Learning to Speak, Speaking to Learn: Research Perspectives on Learner Autonomy Through Collaborative Work in ELT," Carmen Pérez-Llantada describes the project-based, collaborative, and constructivist methodology which she applied to a language course for engineering undergraduates in Spain. Her motivation for conducting this study was to examine ways of improving the motivation and the speaking and listening skills of the students. Her analysis of data from test scores and from learners' written and oral work suggests that the methodology she adopted on this course had a positive impact on learners' attitudes towards learning English. In addition, their proficiency in speaking and listening improved by the end of the academic year.

"Meeting CEF Standards: Research Action in Local Action Research" reports on research conducted in Italy. In this study, Anna Franca Plastina reflects on her role as a teacher educator responsible for mediating between a national action research initiative examining the Common European Framework and a group of teachers who were required to conduct action research in their own classrooms using ideas developed through the national project. Plastina's account of the thinking behind her work with these teachers and the processes she went through in enabling them to experiment with action research in their own classrooms highlights the challenges for her as a teacher educator and for the teachers themselves. This study ultimately provides insights into strategies which teacher educators can use in enabling teachers to become teacher researchers. This account also shows how Plastina's constant reflection on her work allowed her to develop her own professional competence.

In the chapter "Sharing a Journey Towards Success: The Impact of Collaborative Study Groups and CALL in a Legal Context," Alison Riley and Patricia Sours report on an action research project conducted in the context of a legal English course at an Italian university. Informed by theories of motivation and self-determination, they introduced a series of measures to their course, such as self-study groups, with the aim of improving students' levels of participation and performance. The authors' evaluation of the course, using several types of performance and evaluation data, suggests that the support systems which they introduced made a positive difference, as students' levels of participation and their overall performance on the course were better than those of students in previous years.

Linda Taylor's contribution is titled "Aspects of Teacher-Generated Language in the Language Classroom." This study was conducted in the context of preservice teacher education in the UK for teachers of English as a foreign language. Influenced by the fields of classroom discourse, classroom interaction, and language learning tasks, Taylor's motivation in conducting this study was to examine how she and other teachers, in setting up teacher-independent tasks for language learning, used language to manage learning, relate to individuals, and foster interaction in the language classroom. By analyzing audio recordings of language lessons, Taylor identifies several features of the talk teachers use in setting up tasks. She also proposes some rules teacher trainees might use in structuring tasks and enhancing rapport with learners.

In "Do I Talk Too Much? Exploring Dominant and Passive Participation Dynamics," Jennifer E. Thomas reports on a study in which her learners collaborated with her in exploring their oral participation styles. Conducted in a high school in the Czech Republic and drawing on data from questionnaires, learner self-assessments, and Thomas's journal, this study provides insight into what learners think about their own oral participation in the English classroom and how they perceive the participation of their classmates. Thomas was motivated by an awareness that some learners spoke much more than others, and she was keen to understand why this was the case, the extent to which learners were aware of this tendency, and whether making them aware would alter their behaviour. The results indicate that the study made the teacher and the learners more aware of and sensitive to others' perspectives on oral participation.

In another study from Turkey, "Multiple Intelligences Come to the University: A Case Study," Eda Üstünel examines the extent to which multiple intelligences (MI) theory can be applied to content courses on preservice teacher education programmes. Faced with the prospect of teaching a linguistics course to a group of undergraduates, Üstünel documented the processes she went through in designing and implementing a course which reflected the principles of MI theory. Her evaluation of the course, based on data from her own observations, trainees' work, and their end-of-course evaluations, suggests that MI theory can be productively applied to content courses in teacher education contexts. She also acknowledges, though, the demands which working with MI theory placed on her as the teacher educator and on her trainees.

In "Between the Lines: Using Interaction Journals in E-mail Projects," Karin Vogt discusses a project in which German learners of English developed their intercultural competence by corresponding via e-mail with U.S. counterparts. During a period of three months, the German learners reflected on their experiences through interaction journals. By reviewing these journals and the actual e-mails the learners exchanged, Vogt was able to analyse the nature of the intercultural learning that took place. The study provides evidence that interaction journals stimulate intercultural learning. In addition, Vogt provides insight into the processes learners go through in developing intercultural knowledge.

In summary, *Language Teacher Research in Europe* provides evidence of how, through investigating their own practices, English language teaching professionals can deepen their understanding of their work and enhance the learning experiences of the individuals they teach. Despite differences in the particular themes explored and the contexts in which the research was conducted, the contributions presented here are united by a common concern for improving the quality of teaching and learning in TESOL. I hope that the examples of teacher research in this volume provide inspiration and practical ideas for TESOL professionals who share this concern and who want to use research as a way of exploring English language teaching and learning in a principled and contextually relevant manner.

Simon Borg is the editor of Language Teacher Research in Europe. *He is a senior lecturer in TESOL at the School of Education, University of Leeds, England. His research interests are teacher cognition, grammar teaching, and teacher research. His most recent publication is* Teacher Cognition and Language Education *(2006, Continuum).*

CHAPTER 2

Primary School EFL Teachers as Researchers (*Turkey*)

Derin Atay

Probably nothing within a school has more impact on students in terms of skills development, self-confidence, or classroom behavior than the personal and professional growth of teachers. (Barth, 1990, p. 49)

Issue

The 8-year compulsory education system starting in 1997 brought significant changes to foreign language education in Turkey. Under this law it became obligatory for public primary school students to start studying a foreign language in the fourth grade. In 2000, foreign language education in kindergarten and the first three grades of primary education was also officially permitted by the Ministry of Education. As a result of this development, preservice teacher education programmes changed in corresponding ways, in particular by adding a Teaching English to Young Learners course. Little attention, though, has been paid to the needs of practising teachers, and many experienced teachers of English in Turkish state schools have not received specific in-service training relevant to the teaching of young learners.

Some in-service training is provided by the Ministry of Education in Turkey, but this training is infrequent and focuses on generic issues relevant to teachers from different schools and contexts. In these courses, despite an emerging consensus in the teacher education literature about the need to change dominant practices in K–12 teacher professional development (Lieberman & Miller, 2001; Little, 1993; Richardson, 1994), a training model generally unconnected to teachers' daily work continues to persist as the most common form of delivery. Thus, in most in-service training workshops the norm for professional development is that experts expose teachers to new ideas or train them in new practices, paying little attention to the beliefs and knowledge these experienced teachers already have.

To understand the context of the research discussed here, it is important to acknowledge that teachers working in state schools have heavy workloads—27 to 30 hours a week consisting of three or four different classes at different levels. Thus, finding additional time for in-service training is a challenge for most teachers. This chapter reports on my attempt to respond to the limited opportunities for professional development offered to educators teaching English to young learners at state schools in Turkey. Specifically, I provided an in-service course for such teachers, with the primary goal of encouraging them to conduct research into some aspect of their own classrooms.

Background Literature

Teachers need continuing support through professional development because initial teacher education cannot satisfy educators' learning needs throughout their careers. Teachers can benefit from support when preparing for common changes, such as altering a course syllabus or modifying class objectives, just as they can when changing schools, taking on new responsibilities, positioning themselves for promotions, or taking steps to avoid burnout.

The primary way to support teachers in their personal and professional growth is through professional development programmes. The limitations of the previously mentioned training models have in recent years led educational researchers and practitioners to reassess what constitutes professional development (Darling-Hammond, 2003; Lieberman & Miller, 2001). Consequently, there have been many attempts to alter the methods of teacher professional development so that teachers can assume control of classroom decisions and actively participate in their own instructional improvement on an ongoing basis (Knight & Boudah, 1998). From this perspective, rather than relying solely on generalizations or input provided by outside researchers, teachers are encouraged through in-service training to carry out research to resolve problems or to increase their understandings of their individual classes or situations.

Lytle and Cochran-Smith (1990) broadly defined teacher research as "systematic and intentional inquiry carried out by teachers" (p. 83). This definition is consistent not only with the idea that deliberate learning is research but also with the notion that every lesson should be an enquiry for the teacher (Goswami & Stillman, 1987). According to McKernan (1988), teacher research suggests basing professional development on a rigorous examination of one's own teaching practices:

> The idea is that each school, and indeed each classroom, is a laboratory in which the curriculum and problems experienced as problems by teachers (not outside researchers) are subjected to empirical examination by practitioners. (p. 154)

Teacher research invites teachers to question the common assumption that knowledge for and about classroom teaching should be generated at the university and then used in schools, following an *outside-in* approach (Kraft, 2002; Lewin, 1946a; Stenhouse, 1985).

Studies have shown that teacher research as a form of professional development often has a profound effect on those undertaking it, in some cases transforming the classrooms and schools in which they work. Researchers' self-reports have revealed that teacher research facilitates teachers' critical thought (Black, 1996; Day, 1984) and teacher collaboration (Tieg, Bailey, Arllen, & Gable, 1993), boosts teachers' self-esteem and confidence levels (Loucks-Horsley, Hewson, Love, & Stiles, 1998), increases their awareness of students' needs (Soo Hoo, 1993), and helps to create a positive school culture—one that is supportive of teacher reflection and experimentation (Francis, Hirsch, & Rowland, 1994).

Yet many of the references in the literature on the value of teacher research are anecdotal and do not result from systematic and intentional exploration of teachers' experiences (Huberman, 1996). Moreover, there is often little or no information about the specific characteristics of the research experience and context responsible for promoting this growth.

Thus, this chapter intentionally explores the research experiences of Turkish primary school teachers of English. First, I present the context and details of the professional development programme, which provided teachers with relevant theoretical knowledge and guided them to conduct research. Then, I focus on the participating teachers' perspectives on this in-service training programme.

Procedures

The impetus for this study came from informal discussions with heads and teachers at public primary schools when I visited them during the practicum period for student teachers completing studies at my institution, Marmara University in Istanbul. The heads seemed to have the same concerns. They recognized that conditions were not the best but emphasized that we should find a way to motivate, train, develop, and support teachers. In response, I volunteered to conduct an in-service programme for teachers.

When trying to prepare a proposal for the in-service programme during the summer of 2004, I had two major aims in mind: (1) to support teachers' development, and (2) to deepen my understanding of teachers' experiences while engaging in research. I wanted to encourage teachers to carry out their own research without following the *technicist* approach (i.e., studying and applying theories developed by others) that teacher education has taken in several settings. As the facilitator, I would not propose a question for teachers to consider. Instead, teachers would reflect, ground their analyses in their own practices, and examine questions in their own contexts.

I did not want to act as an outside expert. Yet I believed that updating teachers' theoretical knowledge might be necessary for two reasons. First, teaching is connected with choices about what must be taught and how, so teachers need theory when making these choices (Sachs, 2003). Second, teachers should be familiar with relevant concepts and methodology to carry out research.

As I developed this programme and my study, I had to consider the following questions:

- To what extent would the participating teachers be familiar with research?

- Would each teacher accept the role of researcher?

- Would the teachers be willing to reflect on their practices and experiences?

- How could I structure the professional development programme to support and enable teachers to carry out research?

- How could I join my two roles—being a knowledge transmitter and a research guide—in the most effective way?

Moving forward, in the second month of the 2004–2005 academic year I met with 49 teachers working in 14 public schools. I gave them brief information about myself and my plans related to the programme, which would last 6 weeks, with each session running from 2½ to 4 hours. At the outset I made it clear to participants that our collaboration would be part of my personal research focused on improving practices in teacher education programmes, and that they were to carry out their own research. Teachers, therefore, would act as the subjects of research and also as researchers enquiring into their own experiences and practices. After these discussions, 39 teachers—27 female and 12 male—agreed to join the programme provided that I would not give them any extra readings.

Because the schools were located close to one other, we decided to meet in two groups in the afternoons after classes, rotating to different schools each week. For the first meeting, I asked each participating teacher to write a short biography.

SETTINGS AND TEACHER PROFILE

As for the teaching environment, all schools were in a suburb of Istanbul and had 400 to 550 students. The majority of the students were from low-income families. One of the schools was also the professional development school for my university.

In terms of class size, the schools did not differ from each other. Each class had about 35 to 40 students. For English lessons, the schools used the same books, prepared and suggested by the Turkish Ministry of Education.

All of the participating teachers were native speakers of Turkish. The average age of the teachers was just over 31, and their teaching experience averaged just over 9 years. Out of 39 teachers, 21 were English language teaching graduates; 13 were English language and literature graduates; and 5 were graduates of other departments, such as sociology, translation, or chemistry. Twelve of the teachers were not regular teachers at these public schools but rather were working on a contract basis. None of the teachers had a master's degree. Because teacher salaries are very low in Turkey, 15 of the teachers also taught courses for private schools and 5 teachers gave private lessons to students at different levels.

DATA COLLECTION INSTRUMENTS

Data for this study were collected by means of field notes and journals. My field notes helped me document the process of training, and I asked all participating teachers to keep journals of their experiences throughout the programme. The benefits of reflective journal writing have been discussed in the context of in-service teacher training (Jarvis, 1992), and the ongoing personal-professional development of practising teachers (Appel, 1995; Bailey, Curtis, & Nunan, 1998). Borg (2001) has also illustrated the value of journal writing as a tool to support the development of research skills.

In this study, teachers' reflective journal writing provided me with insight into the personal and implicit processes they experienced during their research. The journal data provided the basis of the findings I discuss in this chapter. I analyzed the journals using pattern coding, as suggested by the Miles and Huberman (1994) model of qualitative analysis, to reduce the "large amounts of data into a smaller number of analytic units" (p. 69).

THE IN-SERVICE PROGRAMME

One week after my first meeting with the teachers, the programme started. In planning the course I had decided to focus initially on the professional development experiences of the participating teachers, aiming to find out if a link existed between the theoretical knowledge they had gained from attending various EFL seminars and their own classroom practices. After the teachers introduced themselves in Turkish, I asked them to form groups and discuss a specific issue related to professional development (e.g., the role of researchers vs. the role of teachers, teacher enquiry, reflection) and share their experiences on this issue. Yet I noticed that only a few teachers expressed their views, and the others took notes. With hopes of initiating discussion, I introduced several concepts: *reflection*, *knowledge transmission*, *teacher burnout*, and *teachers' interactive decision making*. Despite my intentions, the session turned into a lecture. The questions I posed about teachers' own experiences did not elicit much discussion because the same people talked all the time.

At the end of the session, I felt that it would be difficult to change the teachers' approaches. Although they had volunteered to participate in the programme, they were hesitant to express themselves, especially in English. (I had told them they could shift to Turkish whenever they wanted.) Most of the participants wrote down every word I said.

In the second week, we moved to the concept of research. Because none of the participants had ever conducted research in the classroom, they could not make much connection between research and effective classroom practice. They generally perceived research as working with computers, learning how to do statistics, and using technical language. I tried to explain the positive effects that conducting research could have on teachers' classroom practices and professional development, and I told them that we could do a small-scale research project together.

With this goal in mind, we watched a 25-minute video filmed in a public school class of young learners. I then asked the teachers to work in pairs to discuss aspects of the teacher's practices that they noticed when watching the video for the second time. For example, the teacher in the recording used only one type of question, a display question, and indicated a student's correct answer only by saying, "Good, thank you." When a student gave an incorrect reply, the teacher frowned and waited for the correct answer from the same student for a short time and then turned to another student. Even if the second student could not come up with the correct answer, the teacher did not say the correct version.

My aim for this task was to find out if the teachers were familiar with different types of questioning and feedback and different learning styles. Some teachers indicated that there was a problem with the teacher's feedback, but they could not offer alternatives. None of them discussed the amount of Turkish vs. English spoken or the lack of visuals in a class of young learners.

As mentioned previously, my goal was for teachers' needs to direct the flow and content of the sessions. At this point they seemed to need more information about the issues they had watched on the video, so we talked about different types of feedback.

In the third session, I continued providing them with information on different questioning types, learning styles and strategies, and issues related to classroom management. When I was preparing for that session, I was afraid that the whole time would be spent lecturing. Yet, contrary to my expectations, teachers asked questions, gave examples from their own experiences, and shared their concerns with one another.

In the fourth session, I asked the teachers to think of a topic that interested them for their research. The following concerns came up:

- My students don't like English; they are so demotivated.

- I want to observe another teacher's class.

- My students don't read anything in English.

- How can I make my students speak English in class?

- My students want me to translate every single word into Turkish.

Sharing these problems with the group was a good opportunity for reflection and collaboration for teachers. When a teacher indicated a problem, many other teachers added to the issue by discussing their own experiences.

Next I introduced various data collection instruments which could be used for the research topics they had identified. I knew that a lack of time and certain research skills would be highly constraining, so to overcome these constraints I told the teachers they would not have to spend time devising any data instruments if they did not want to. I showed them authentic examples of an audio recording, a diary, a questionnaire, an interview, and observation instruments. In this way teachers not only became familiar with the uses of various data collection instruments but also became sensitive to the issues, problems, and questions which might be related to their own research. Finally, together we conducted a simple analysis of an anxiety inventory (an example of quantitative data) and of an interview and a diary (examples of qualitative data). At the end of this session, I asked the teachers to begin researching a topic of their choice. I told them that they could e-mail me if they had any questions, and I reminded them to keep journals throughout the process.

The last two weeks of the programme were spent on teachers' research. During this time, teachers shared their topics and concerns with one another and with me, and they reflected on the process.

Two weeks after the programme ended, teachers submitted their research projects and journals. Out of 39 teachers, only 12 submitted their reports and their journals, and 27 (some of whom had started but could not finish their research) handed in only their journals. Nine teachers carried out collaborative research projects, focusing on the same topic and sharing and comparing their results with another teacher. Most of the teachers said that they had started their research but could not finish because of their workload.

Results

The results I discuss here come from the journals the teachers kept during the programme. From a qualitative analysis of these journals, I identified four major themes, each of which was further broken down into subthemes, as described in Table 1. I now discuss each theme in turn, illustrating the discussion with quotations from the teachers' journals, some of which have been translated from Turkish.

RESEARCH PROCESS

Most of the journal responses within the research process theme referred to ways in which the teachers wanted to improve their teaching practices. In the following extract,[1] for example, the teacher comments on the discovery that collecting data from learners could make a positive contribution to understanding them and hence to teaching them more effectively:

> Whenever I ask my students to do an activity in pairs, most of them ignore my remark and do the task on their own. I told them what pair-work means so many times, both in English and in Turkish. . . . This morning I told the class that I want to discuss something with them, and asked them whether they liked pair-work or not. First, their reaction was neutral. They avoided giving clear yes/no answers; instead there were some vague responses like "Sometimes I like it," "When it's in the fifth hour I don't like it," "We do our best. We speak English . . . what else?" When I insisted, a few students said that they found pair-work activities "childish" and "artificial," i.e., talking to their Turkish friends in English seemed very funny. Yet the majority was silent, so it was

Table 1. Summary of Coding for Teachers' Journals

Major Theme	Subthemes
Research process	Attempts to improve teaching practice Raised awareness Sharing results with wider community
Collaboration	Feedback on teaching practices Support of the instructor Opportunities for collaborative reflection
Personal outcomes	Increased sense of professionalism Renewed enthusiasm about teaching
Challenges	Worries about time constraints Worries about implementation Problems with collaboration

difficult for me to have a clear understanding of their attitudes. . . . Today I asked my students to write down their opinions whether they found pair-work necessary and functional to improve their English. . . . Written responses surprisingly were different from my expectations. Besides telling their opinions, they had also written their suggestions on the use of pair-work in class: "I would talk more in a pair-work activity if you helped us with the vocabulary," "It is difficult for me to speak in English because when I lack the necessary vocabulary, I shift to Turkish," "I had never thought interviews or question-naires could be considered as part of real research." This morning I told them that I read what they had written. I also told them that I was going to put the target words on the [overhead projector] provided that they use them. It seems to work but we'll see.

Another teacher similarly reflected on how, by asking her learners about their attitudes toward reading, she found out that a key problem for them was a lack of access to books in English outside of school:

Today I gave them the attitude questionnaire I prepared. It has only five ques-tions. . . . I counted the answers and found out that most of my students do not like reading in English because they think they would not understand anything. The majority of them do not have any English readers at home. They would not ask their parents to buy English books because the English books are very expensive. If given a chance they would like to read classics, autobiographies, and books on wars.

In response to these findings, the teacher brought books in English to the class-room and allowed learners to borrow them.

Also common in the teachers' journals were reflections on how conducting research, in particular classroom observations, raised their awareness of issues in teaching and learning. The following journal extract (names used are pseudo-nyms) captures this connection between classroom observation and awareness of teaching:

Today I met with Feza and we decided to use the observation form we dis-cussed in the session. . . . The major thing I learned from this observation is the importance of having a positive relationship with one's students. Of course I knew it before, but it is probably the first time when I really saw it from another perspective. I was in Feza's class sitting among students. Whenever she asked a question, students sitting next to me were whispering the answers to each other but not raising their hands. Only three or four students in the front were volunteering. After a while, I asked the students in the back "You know the answer. Why don't you raise your hands?" One of them said, "Yes, but if it's wrong, Mrs. Aysan will get very angry with us." Students in Feza's class were afraid [of] her. I could not imagine something like this because she is such a wonderful person. . . . I made up my mind: I'll find out how my students feel in my class, because there are many who are hesitant to communicate in English.

The third subtheme relating to the research process concerned sharing research findings with a wider community. This issue was mentioned by only a minority of teachers, but their concerns reflected more general views held in Turkey about the prestige attached to publication. The following extract reflects such views but also acknowledges the challenges involved:

I have interesting data about my students' attitudes towards learning English now. Carrying out research and getting my paper published in a Turkish journal has been one of [my] dreams. I know it's hard and requires professional work, but who knows?

COLLABORATION

The first subtheme under collaboration was the positive effects of collaborative feedback on teachers' classroom practices. In the following extract, the teacher comments on how collaborative observation and discussion as part of the research process allowed him to identify a feature of his work:

Sami today asked me whether we could videotape each other's class and discuss it later. I don't like being observed, forget about being filmed. . . . It wasn't as bad as I expected. The students had fun, especially in the first 10 minutes [when] they were waving at the camera, smiling, etc. . . . When discussing the lesson today, Sami told me that I was directing the questions to the whole class but only choosing students among the volunteers. So at the end I was dealing with the same three. . . . When you work with someone, [you can] share alternatives and get aware of a problem which might otherwise be unnoticed.

A second subtheme under collaboration was the role that support from the trainer played in enabling the teachers to make progress with their research. Many comments touched on this issue, and some teachers even felt that without this support they would not be able to continue doing research once the in-service programme was over:

I think I will go on looking for more things to read, but when you are not here I doubt it. I should thank you for this. How can I go to the library and do the search and find all this stuff on my own?

The third subtheme under collaboration was the value teachers assigned to opportunities to share ideas. The following comments illustrate their appreciation:

I have taught alone for many years now, and I don't ever get feedback about my teaching. I liked the way we exchanged ideas.

Through discussing with him why I did particular things, why the departmental policy was so and such, I was actually analyzing for myself and evaluating for myself . . . which made me look at: "Well, is this really the best way of doing it?"

Me, Tuba, and Gokçe were really an effective team. I wish we [could] keep seeing each other. It was great to think [up] solutions to the problems we had.

PERSONAL OUTCOMES

The third major theme to emerge from teachers' journals related to the personal outcomes they felt they had achieved through the course. The following comments highlight an increased sense of professionalism:

I feel enriched since the beginning of the programme. What I've always kept in my mind as theory has been put into practice. What I learned about reflection, collaboration, and observation has been put into practice.

Today I handed in my project to the head—I couldn't find the trainer. I felt proud (a feeling which I had forgotten for some time). I felt I've made a contribution to the field.

I know it may not be considered real, serious research maybe, but I feel as if I have achieved something professionally.

Similarly, many teachers commented that doing research had given them a renewed sense of enthusiasm for teaching:

I have taught for 18 years. Sometimes you lose sight of some very important aspects in dealing with your students. Selma was so positive, so energetic, and so enthusiastic that I found it contagious.

Collaborating with another teacher kept me awake. . . . Actually having to think about why you are doing something and where it is going and that sort of thing, I find very stimulating.

CHALLENGES

The final major theme emerging from the teachers' journals related to the challenges they encountered while doing research. A key issue was time, because some of the teachers were not released from any of their usual duties in order to do the research:

I think it's too much to ask. With all these working hours and students. . . . Actually I really like doing research in my own way, but now it seems impossible.

I have a teaching load of 21 hours in two different schools and I teach a private course. When am I supposed to do research? And is it worth [the effort]?

Comments also related to the difficulties teachers had in deciding what to research for their projects and how to go about it:

I have some questions in my mind, but I can't verbalize them appropriately.

I have doubts about this research project. I don't know if I can find any topic to investigate. I don't have any problems. . . . Today I discussed this issue with the others; they were lost too. I need more guidance.

Well, I'm lost. I can't analyze all these things. What should I do? Group them or count the answers one by one? I wish you spent more time with us. I don't feel like asking everything through e-mails.

Some teachers also believed that the collaborative requirements of research were not achievable:

When we started the research, everything was great. But when it came to writing down all we had done, nobody volunteered. There was some kind of tension, and [then] the research was over.

I wonder how often can we find to do all that? How often can [we] team up with other teachers when the training is over?

At first I thought working in a group would make things easier. But now I [have] realized that it's much more difficult. We can't arrange our times, and Arzu has changed the appointments so many times that I got bored with the whole process.

Inevitably, the process was not an entirely positive one for all the teachers in the programme.

Reflection

In this study I worked with a group of teachers on a professional development programme which encouraged the participants to do research. Teachers were busy, working under difficult and less than satisfactory conditions. The prospect of launching into the realm of researcher, on top of the many things that a teacher already does, probably seemed intimidating to them at the beginning. Despite the dropouts and irregular attendance of some teachers, most were able to start a research project, with a smaller number actually completing it.

In considering how the programme enabled teachers to think about and do research, I believe that a number of characteristics were important. Firstly, the teachers were volunteers who felt a need for personal and professional growth. Secondly, the programme content was tailored to their needs. I was highly flexible with the content, and the teachers felt it. Thirdly, throughout the programme we maintained a positive atmosphere. I knew that after a day's teaching the teachers were tired, and I continually tried to show my appreciation for their participation. I believe that if the teachers were given some time off, the process would be even more effective. Finally, although they had an active role in their research, I directed them through the process. Direction in this programme was different from the traditional transfer models, in which the facilitator transfers theory via instruction and the teacher is expected to apply the theory. My guidance was process oriented, and teachers knew that I was not trying to impose things on them. I repeatedly indicated that they knew their own context much better than I did.

Most of the teachers benefited from research and collaboration. Although many indicated that they could not see the changes they were expecting as a result of their research, the research did enable them to question many things in their own contexts and understand the relationship between their beliefs and classroom practices. Many commented that their experiences in becoming a researcher had changed their ways of teaching and approaching the students. Others discussed the value of a collaborative research process, which allowed them to share ideas, listen to each other, and contribute suggestions and ideas.

The fact that only 12 teachers submitted their research has implications for future studies. Future professional development courses need to be more coordinated; that is, permissions should be received to provide teachers with release time to do research. For the majority of teachers, time constraints and difficulties in scheduling activities during the day because of full or inconsistent classroom schedules were major obstacles. For these reasons, some teachers attended only sporadically, and five teachers withdrew from the course.

The role of the instructor merits further consideration, too. I should have provided the teachers with more follow-up support during the research process. If provided with more guidance, particularly on the data analysis section, more teachers may have submitted their reports. But my own workload, along with the high number of participating teachers, kept me from providing this level of support.

The goal of this teacher research was to enable teachers to shift from teaching as telling to teaching as listening and learning. I believe that most of the participating teachers have begun the journey. They came to view teacher research as a process of changing or becoming transformed themselves as a means to facilitate effective practices for their students. The fact that four teachers from the course applied for the master's programme at my university indicates that thinking about and doing research has, for some of the teachers at least, stimulated an interest in further professional development.

Derin Atay teaches at Marmara University, Istanbul, Turkey.

Note

1. Journal entries from different days have been combined in the extracts.

CHAPTER 3

Teaching Web-Mediated EAP to Ethnic Minority Students (*UK*)

Mihye Harker and Dimitra Koutsantoni

Issue

In higher education institutions in the UK the term "home students" is used to describe individuals who are resident in the UK. Even though this term suggests homogeneity, home students in fact include students from a diverse range of backgrounds. In particular, a significant proportion of home students come from ethnic minority backgrounds representing diversity in terms of their culture and religion, the languages they speak, the length of time they have lived in Britain, and many other aspects. To some of these students English is their first language, but to others it is an additional language. Likewise, to some of them Britain is their birthplace, but to others it is their adopted country.

In the context of higher education, this particular group of students often needs support with the academic English skills required to follow university courses in their chosen disciplines. This chapter focuses on this issue. In particular, we describe and evaluate a project intended to develop the academic English writing skills of ethnic minority undergraduates at a British university.

Background Literature

Previous research results have highlighted ethnic minority students' needs related to academic writing in English (Bhattacharyya, Ison, & Blair, 2003; Connor, La Valle, Tackey, & Perryman, 1996; Connor, Tyers, Davis, Tackey, & Modood, 2003), detailing the reported underachievement of such students (Connor et al., 2003) and the resulting likelihood of them withdrawing from their studies (Patrick, 2001). This issue of providing help for students from ethnic minority backgrounds is therefore an essential one in the context of higher education in the UK.

In our context, the issue of providing help with academic communication skills for ethnic minority students was particularly crucial because we were teacher researchers at one of the new (post-1992) universities in the UK, which have a higher proportion of ethnic minority students. Ethnic minority students comprise an estimated 15% of all undergraduates in higher education institutions and are concentrated in a relatively small number of institutions, mainly the modern (post-1992) universities in London and other big cities, where they make up more than 30% of undergraduates (Bhattacharyya et al., 2003; Pathak, 2000). University of Luton is no exception and admits more than the regional average for ethnic minorities.

Many members of this diverse group of British ethnic minority students are aware of the support they require with academic English. In a preparatory survey we conducted, teaching staff at Luton confirmed that a considerable number of ethnic minority students urgently need help with their English for academic purposes (EAP) skills. To meet these needs, the English for Excellence (EfE) project, jointly funded by the university and the Higher Education European Social Fund, was launched. The EfE project's goal was to provide instruction in academic communication skills for students from ethnic minority backgrounds to increase their academic success and their retention in higher education.

Several studies (Chen, Belkada, & Okamoto, 2004; Jarvis, 2001, 2004; Stapleton, 2003) have reported on the advantages of teaching and learning EAP courses in a Web-mediated environment. Therefore, to accommodate student diversity and to provide flexible learning modes, we as programme developers chose the Web as the medium of instruction. Web-based instruction allowed the EAP learning programme to be offered in the classroom (as a type of blended learning) and by distance; other benefits included time flexibility, ability to facilitate student-centred learning, increased access to materials, reinforced learning, privacy, ability to repeat tasks, and wealth of information (Felix, 2001).

This chapter focuses on our work with the first cohort of students participating in the EfE learning programme through blended learning (combining Web-based materials and in-class instruction, as defined in Osguthorpe and Graham, 2003). Mihye Harker worked as project researcher for EfE, and Dimitra Koutsantoni taught EAP at the University of Luton. Our aims in doing this research were to evaluate the experience of this first cohort, to gain insights into their perspectives on the course we prepared and taught, and to identify points to address in implementing this course with subsequent cohorts of students.

Procedures

Once the sponsors decided on the main strategy of providing tutoring to the target students, we began developing the course materials, informed by students' learning needs and target needs (Hutchinson & Waters, 1987). As stated previously, we needed to address the issue of supporting students from ethnic minority backgrounds in developing their academic English skills, particularly their writing skills.

WEB-BASED INSTRUCTION

We chose the Web as the medium of instruction because it offered several advantages. Specifically, we valued its flexibility in presenting the project's optional courses, acknowledging that students might not necessarily find time to be in the classroom for a non-credit-bearing course. Easy access to the learning materials and the ability to repeat tasks were also considered great advantages. In addition, previous research (Felix, 2001) had noted student interest in the medium, and most prospective participants at our university confirmed their interest during preparatory interviews we conducted.

Although the Web allowed the programme to be delivered in the form of blended learning in the classroom or at a distance, distance learning presented further challenges in planning the course content and presentation. In other words, working on lessons without a teacher's immediate help could pose difficulties for students. We therefore took the distance students into account when planning the content and presentation of the learning materials.

LEARNING MATERIALS

In the early stages, we decided the programme would focus on improving written communication skills because interviews with target students and staff revealed this as one of the areas needing the most attention.

With that focus in mind, we grouped the learning materials under various themes such as organising essays; writing effective paragraphs; referencing; and employing caution, certainty, and attitude in academic writing. Each lesson addressed one theme. We also organised additional tutorials under specific skills such as grammar, academic writing, and academic vocabulary. The Web site which presented the material also included learning support features that allowed students to save their work, make personal notes, and give feedback on lessons and tutorials. The Web site facilitated communication between the tutor and learners and among the learners via a chat feature that allowed them to leave messages or discuss material, and via a noticeboard that let tutors post messages to students.

RECRUITMENT AND PARTICIPANTS

Programme participants were volunteers we recruited from the target group. In the initial stages, recruitment mainly involved publicising the programme through the teaching staff, putting up posters in prominent places on campus, and creating the project Web site. We used interviews with students and staff as a means of publicising the programme, gauging instructional needs, and diagnosing common problem areas in academic writing.

Thirty volunteers participated in the programme as the first cohort (excluding those who signed up but failed to attend class). As Table 1 shows, participants were diverse in terms of their discipline studied, ethnicity, age, degree level, and languages used.

THE PROGRAMME

The programme was taught over the course of 9 weeks, with one 2-hour session each week.

First session and pretest. The first session was longer than subsequent ones because it included a 45-minute pretest at the beginning. This diagnostic pretest consisted of two parts: reading and summarising, and writing a short argumentative essay on a given topic. Because the participants were from various disciplines, we chose a topic of general interest for both parts. For the reading and summarising part, students read a 218-word passage and then summarised the passage in one to three sentences. For the writing part, they wrote an essay of up to 400 words. Their tests were double-marked on a 3-point scale for the summarising part and a 5-point scale for the essay part. In-between grades such as 2.5 were allowed in case there was difficulty in deciding a clear-cut grade. We returned the tests to the students before the second class, with detailed feedback on writing style (strengths and weaknesses) and areas for improvement.

Lesson structure. Each class session evolved around a theme: academic writing style; organising essays; writing effective paragraphs; referencing and

Table 1. Diversity of the Participants

Discipline	Ethnicity	Age	Degree Level	Languages Used
12 disciplines	9 different ethnic backgrounds	20–47	Undergraduate (16) Postgraduate (14)	17 different languages

bibliographies; tenses and adverbs; caution, certainty, and attitude in academic writing; paraphrasing and summarising; and academic vocabulary. At the end of each session, participants were asked to leave feedback focusing on two points, the most and least useful component of the lesson. They were also asked to write an argumentative essay as an assignment each week. Students could choose from a variety of topics concerning current affairs. According to the topic they chose, they were required to discuss causes and effects, to compare and contrast, to define or explain a concept, to conduct small scale research and report the results, to argue a point of view, or to suggest solutions to problems. The tutor returned each piece of homework to the student with detailed feedback recommending areas for further work.

Posttest. On completion of the programme, participants took an achievement test which consisted of the same two parts as the pretest and which was marked on the same scale as before. They had to read and summarise a 166-word passage and write an argumentative essay.

Questionnaires. The participants also answered questionnaires asking for their opinions of various aspects of the Web site and the learning programme.

Follow-up interviews. Finally, follow-up phone interviews investigated the positive effects of the programme on students' coursework. These interviews consisted of the following questions:

- Have you been able to apply what you learnt on the EfE programme on your degree coursework?

- Which particular things that you have learnt have been especially beneficial to your degree studies? Try to be as specific as possible.

- Have your grades improved or have you received more positive feedback from your tutors on your assignments as a result of your participation on the programme?

Results

The findings from the study pertain to two aspects: student achievement in the programme and effectiveness of the programme as evaluated by students' formative, summative, and follow-up feedback. Although 30 students started the course, only 21 completed it. Students' achievements and feedback are based on the completers only, except for formative feedback. In discussing these results, we focus on understanding how the course was evaluated by the students.

STUDENT ACHIEVEMENT

Students' progress was evaluated through a comparison of the completers' pretest and posttest grades. Their posttest grades showed a slight improvement from their pretest grades for both sections. The average pretest grade for the reading and summarising section rose from 2 to 2.4, which was statistically significant (Wilcoxon Signed Ranks test used). The average posttest grade for the writing section rose from 3.4 to 3.8. Amid the overall upward trend of the posttest grades, improvement tended to be greater for students who attended the course regularly. For instance, one student whose attendance rate was 100% raised his grade from 2.5 to 4 in the writing section. In contrast, students whose attendance was low did not show as much improvement. This trend seems to confirm that students' achievements largely depended on their level of commitment to the course.

EFFECTIVENESS OF THE PROGRAMME

We assessed the effectiveness of the programme through the formative feedback students provided at the end of each lesson and the summative feedback they gave at the end of the course. In addition, we gathered follow-up feedback from students to investigate the usefulness of the course in their respective disciplines.

Formative Feedback

Students' feedback at the end of every lesson showed their overall satisfaction with the lessons. When asked to specify the least useful component in the lesson, many of them answered "nothing" or "everything was useful." On average, about three instances of negative feedback were received in contrast to eight instances of positive feedback in each lesson. In the following examples of positive feedback, students commented about the most useful component in the lesson:

- The different ways in which I can introduce or break one paragraph into different topics

- How to identify linking words and how to write a good, clear, concise paragraph

- Very informative about the knowledge of writing references; very clearly structured

- One-to-one attention from lecturers

- Different ways of expressing certainty/uncertainty, the exercise where we replaced inappropriate phrases with more academic ones

Negative feedback, or comments about the least useful component, included the following:

- Least useful was to find the personal bits in the texts, because I felt it was so obvious.

- The group work. I didn't have the chance to contribute because am not very good on thinking fast.

- The complicated nature of the paragraphs we had to restructure.

- We should talk more about the differences between informal and formal text.

This feedback was particularly useful in gauging students' interests in each lesson. Their quick responses to learning points helped us decide which points to expand on, elaborate on, modify, shorten, or even remove for later cohorts. For instance, we added more exercises on paragraph organisation after some students requested these.

Students' positive feedback also revealed that they had liked tutors' personal attention and the opportunity to perform exercises to reinforce particular learning points. Some of the negative feedback informed us which types of classroom activities students did not enjoy and which they would like to have instead. In addition, difficulty arose when different students responded in a conflicting manner to the same points. For example, on the lesson on referencing, many students answered that they had learnt a great deal and asked for more exercises to practise, but a few students stated that they had not needed a whole lesson devoted to referencing because they already knew enough. This problem seems to reflect students' different learning levels, which can be a challenge in this type of course. Our solution was to keep the lessons as they were and add more advanced exercises for the more advanced students.

Summative Feedback

Participants gave feedback on the course after its completion by answering two questionnaires. One questionnaire concentrated on the functionality and contents of the Web site and the other on the programme. The Web site functionality was positively evaluated by the respondents, with 77% finding it easy to use, 58% finding it working well, and 92% finding the instructions easy to follow. The layout and the presentation of information on the Web site were positively assessed by 69% and 100% of the students respectively.

Some students who expressed negative views about the Web site explained their answers. They stated that the Web site was not easy to use because it had too many sections and the organisation was not easy to follow. Their comments were that it was sometimes slow, that it timed out, that sometimes pages were not displayed, or that there were problems with the server. Some students would have preferred that the Web site follow the order of activities in class, and some wanted more exercises.

When asked to suggest possible changes, students indicated that they would change the current layout, make the aims and objectives of each lesson clearer, and arrange the activities in a more logical way, following the way they were presented in class.

The questionnaire responses also indicated that, on the whole, students were satisfied with the course, felt that the course met their needs, and believed that they received a good standard of teaching in good facilities. Students answered that the course had met their expectations either fully (45%) or to a certain degree (40%). The few who felt that their expectations had not been fully met expected more contact hours, one-to-one meetings with tutors, and help with individual problems.

All of the respondents felt that they had learnt useful academic skills. In terms of the learning materials, 95% of the students indicated that they found the materials useful, and participants described them as detailed, informative, to the point, and in conjunction with their expectations. The classes and the teaching methods were rated useful by 85% of the students, who described them as helpful and comprehensible. Students also indicated that they liked the combination of modern technology and face-to-face teaching. They appreciated the availability of the teaching materials online for independent study outside the class.

All of the respondents found the feedback they received on their homework constructive, and they said it was detailed, easy to understand, and helped them identify weak points and avoid similar mistakes. When asked how they would change the programme if they had the chance, students said they would make the programme last longer. Some also suggested that it could be attended by distance (which was part of the plan but not the case with this first cohort), and others suggested changing the Web site layout.

Participants' responses to both questionnaires revealed that most of them had positive learning experiences and had acquired what they had intended on the course.

Follow-Up Feedback

Students' responses in the follow-up phone interviews (19 interviews out of 21 completers) also showed their satisfaction with the course. When asked whether they had been able to apply what they had learnt to their degree coursework, 17 students answered "yes" or "to some extent." The remaining two students attributed their negative responses to the particular features of their coursework. One of the two said that he had not had the chance to apply what he had learnt because his degree coursework was studio practice. When asked which particular things had been especially beneficial to their degree studies, students mentioned formal/informal styles and referencing (seven respondents), essay structuring (five respondents), grammar (three respondents), and hedging (two respondents). When asked whether their grades had improved or they had received more positive feedback from their tutors on their assignments since the course, six students said "yes." One of them stated that his tutor had said that he had not expressed himself properly in his assignments before the course but that he had improved a great deal since. Two students, however, said "no," and another two were not sure because their grades did not entirely depend on academic English. Seven students had not received their results yet. Two thought that the question was not applicable to them. It was too early to decide whether participation in the course had a long-term positive effect. But students' responses suggest that they had learnt useful skills which were largely applicable to their academic work and that these skills might contribute to their academic achievements, which might in turn help them remain in higher education and complete their studies.

Reflection

SUMMARY OF RESULTS

Student achievement tests showed improvement in academic writing performance in comparison with the diagnostic tests. Their formative feedback on each lesson informed the teachers of their favourable or negative responses to certain tasks and learning points and their perception of relevance of the tasks and learning points to their needs. This formative feedback provided reference points for modifications of the course content for later cohorts. Students' summative feedback through questionnaires showed their overall satisfaction with the programme in relation to the course content, functionality of the Web site, usefulness of the learning support facilities on the Web site, and so on. Students' attitudes towards the learning technology employed on the course were favourable as well. Their responses in the follow-up phone interviews suggest that the course might have a long-term favourable effect on their degree studies.

PROBLEMS ENCOUNTERED DURING THE STUDY

Although students' feedback and their achievements on the course draw a positive picture, a number of problems were encountered while preparing and delivering the course instruction.

First of all, we had problems recruiting voluntary participants. The strategies used were mainly recruiting by word of mouth through teaching staff, publicising through posters, participating in the induction week, and posting information on the project Web site. These proved somewhat useful, but we found it hard to target the right audiences (it was hard to single out the target students). As a result, the first cohort did not reach the target number of 40 participants. Phone calls targeting the right audiences to invite them to participate would have been much more effective. This strategy was in fact employed for the later cohorts and proved very effective. Requesting teaching staff's help to refer students from the target group who might benefit from the course would have been useful as well.

Keeping up participants' commitment levels also proved to be a major challenge. Attendance rates (on average 56%), homework submission rates (on average 11%), and course completion rates (70%) all tended to be low. In particular, the low attendance and course completion rates were a great disappointment and were demoralising to us. The reasons the students provided for not attending or completing the course indicated that these low rates had very much to do with their priorities. Because the course did not award any credits and was optional, it did not seem to be a high priority for the participants. Most students attributed their lack of completion to their degree course workload and said they intended to complete the course after they had addressed more urgent degree work. Because accrediting the course is beyond our control, a more practical solution to these problems would be finding ways to engage students further. Providing additional weekly tutorials (either group or one-to-one) and personal attention might engage and motivate them. Encouraging interaction between students might help retention by providing more social motivation. Adding sections such as self-assessment at the end of each lesson might also help students keep track of their learning and thereby motivate them to stay in the course.

During the preparation stage of the course, we encountered problems with the type of interview questions employed. For instance, an open-ended question about weaknesses with academic English proved slightly problematic. Many (48%) were not able to identify or articulate their specific problems in their academic writing. It would therefore have been much more effective if we had employed a multiple-choice format with some space for individual contributions. We rectified this in later interviews, and the new format proved to be more effective.

Some organisational aspects of the course also proved to be problematic. For example, giving the pretest in the first session caused problems. Many students were not able to relax and felt pressure to complete the tasks. In addition, the classroom was very hot, and many students complained of the inadequate room temperature control. Finally, a few students lost unfinished work because the pretest did not have a save option. Then they had to repeat the tasks, which undoubtedly frustrated them. Giving students the pretest before the lessons began would have helped create a more relaxed atmosphere. In addition, by receiving feedback on their writing before the course began, students might have felt more motivated to tackle their weaknesses during the course.

Certain aspects of the lesson layout did not prove effective. Students were sometimes instructed to jump from one tutorial to another or to follow links, which they seemed to find slightly confusing. Sorting this out inevitably wasted some valuable time in class. It would have been helpful to have a more straightforward layout of each lesson. Furthermore, although we made every attempt to make the learning materials self-explanatory and clear, some students still encountered misunderstanding or confusion during the lessons. In hindsight, we realised that a handbook would have been helpful for reference, and we have since developed one and distributed it to students in later cohorts.

WHAT WE LEARNED

The findings of the study suggest that many British home students from ethnic minority backgrounds need help with their academic English skills, even when English is their first language. The findings could be beneficial for educators establishing an EAP or academic literacies course with ethnically, linguistically, and culturally diverse groups of students. For instance, the findings about students' attitudes towards the use of the Web, the personalised help teachers could provide online and offline, and the role teachers can play in students' motivation, achievement, and retention could be of use to EAP and academic literacy educators. Of similar value is the feedback students gave on content, types of tasks, Web site functions, and online communication avenues. We hope our findings will also be useful to researchers further investigating ways to improve the academic communication skills of home and international students.

On a professional level, this research experience taught us invaluable lessons about our teaching. In particular, the problem of retention (represented by low course completion rates) of the first cohort reminded us of the importance of making a good impression with the first lesson. We also noted the need to have an uncomplicated layout for learning materials, to promote interaction between the teacher and students and among students, and to provide personal attention to individual students in and beyond the Web-mediated classroom. These findings laid the foundation for considerable improvements in retention rates that we achieved in later cohorts.

This experience also helped us learn more about conducting research. First of all, we learned the importance of preparation and attention to detail in research design. Careful preparation and good interview skills proved to be essential for conducting interviews and questionnaires. We found that question type and wording also need attention in order to draw out appropriate responses and avoid confusion. Modifying the research design progressively helped us cater to developing situations. Writing progressive reports and making notes as issues came up proved to be useful in building data for final evaluations. In particular, progressive evaluation proved to be vital in analysing data and evaluating the outcome. These strategies helped build up the complete picture without losing any crucial points at each stage. We also found it essential to be well informed about relevant literature because these resources helped with comparisons, refining our research design, and drawing meaningful conclusions from the data to improve future learning.

Mihye Harker is an independent researcher and interpreter for Cambridgeshire Interpreting and Translation Service (CINTRA) in Cambridge, England. Dimitra Koutsantoni works in Research Development at City University, London, UK.

CHAPTER 4

Are You Doing Well in English? A Study of Secondary School Students' Self-Perceptions (*Hungary*)

Judit Heitzmann

Issue

Why do students behave as they do? How can teachers understand them and scaffold their learning process? These are some of the daily questions that teachers ask themselves. As a practising secondary school teacher of English as a foreign language (EFL), I also often face problems of how to arouse and maintain students' interest and how to provide a suitable learning environment. My desire to understand students' attitudes has strengthened over the years, and, although the research articles that I have read so far have clarified some theoretical issues, a continuous reflection on my own teaching practice has posed further questions.

In the past decade, the role of the learner has become a major focus of research attention, resulting in an increase in studies concentrating on learner variables. Different researchers examine different characteristics of the individual, but attention to major attributes such as language aptitude, motivation, anxiety, self-confidence, learning strategies, and learning styles is prevalent (e.g., Gardner & MacIntyre, 1992, 1993; Oxford & Ehrman, 1993; Skehan, 1989). Other authors (e.g., Horwitz, 1987; White, 1999; Williams & Burden, 1999) highlight the causal relationships between learners' beliefs and expectations on the one hand, and the actual strategies they use while learning the foreign language on the other. Based on their findings, Williams and Burden go even further and suggest that teachers play a significant role in forming the learning environment, and thus have a considerable impact on learners' beliefs. They argue that in an achievement-oriented school, for example, students will most probably set performance goals for themselves rather than learning goals, and their perceptions of success and failure will be based on marks and examination results. This, however, will not foster their ability to become effective, successful learners.

Those ideas suggested by Williams and Burden (1999) inspired me to replicate and extend their research and investigate a group of my own students. My aim was to obtain insight into students' thoughts and feelings by discovering what factors they attribute to their successes and failures in learning English. By comparing the results with previous findings, I wanted to see whether the same picture would arise in a Hungarian setting, that is, whether students in an achievement-oriented Hungarian school conceptualised success the same way as the participants of the Williams and Burden study. Another goal was to see how I, as a teacher researcher, could utilise the results in the classroom for the sake of the students' progress—in simpler terms, how could I, through this research, become a better teacher?

In what follows, first I define the constructs that provide the theoretical background for the study. After a detailed description of the research method, I discuss the results in light of the research questions. I then interpret the findings and provide a summary of the conclusions drawn from the investigations.

Background Literature

LEARNER BELIEFS

Learners' and teachers' beliefs concerning foreign language learning have been the focus of interest for the past two decades. The reason for this attention is manifold. First, researchers have found that beliefs help individuals understand different situations and therefore adapt to new environments (Abelson, 1979; Lewis, 1990). Second, beliefs play an essential role in defining tasks, and they influence people's behaviour (Bandura, 1986; Nespor, 1987; Schommer, 1990). Third, according to White (1999), expectations, which may affect individuals' reactions to a new environment, are also determined by beliefs. Adopting the term "mental constructions of experience" from Sigel (1985), White defines beliefs as "mental constructions of experience that are held to be true and that guide behaviour" (p. 443). Learners' belief systems help them see what is expected of them and act accordingly.

In line with these analyses, Horwitz (1987) underscores the importance of understanding the nature of student beliefs, suggesting that these beliefs have an impact on the choice and use of appropriate learning strategies, on students' behaviour in the classroom, and ultimately on learners' acquisition of language. As a further step, Horwitz suggests a comparison of student and teacher beliefs, which, in her view, may help reveal potential clashes as well as explain why certain students lose confidence in the teaching approach.

PERCEIVED REASONS FOR SUCCESS

Williams and Burden (1999) narrow the scope of belief research and investigate students' perceived reasons for their successes and failures. Claiming that these factors are accountable for the success of the whole learning process, they describe two theories that provide a better understanding of how students see themselves as language learners.

The first theory, constructivism, is based on the view that absolute knowledge does not exist. Individuals understand things in different ways and construct their own personal meanings. Learners' self-conceptions are at the centre of the learning process, because it is these aspects that influence how individuals make sense of their learning as well as their attitude towards the learning task. These self-conceptions include notions such as (a) self-concept, which refers to people's overall view of themselves (Wylie, 1979); (b) self-efficacy, which shows how competent learners see themselves in a particular field (Bandura, 1977); and (c) locus of control, which shows whether or not people consider the events in their lives to be within their control (Wang, 1983).

The second theory, which is essentially also constructivist in nature, is attribution theory. It takes a step further by directly focusing on how individuals perceive and understand successes and failures in their lives. In his seminal work, Weiner (1986) asserts that the causes to which people attribute outcomes in achievement tasks can be viewed in three dimensions: (1) locus of causality, which shows whether individuals see their successes and failures as caused by themselves or by others; (2) stability, showing whether the attribute is fixed or changeable; and (3) controllability, which refers to the extent to which an outcome is within the control of the individual.

On the other hand, Williams and Burden (1999) broaden the range of factors which explain success and failure, thus providing a more precise definition of the construct. In their interpretation, attributions cluster around such notions as internal feelings, developmental stages, external influences and social contexts. At the same time, they emphasise the importance of understanding how external influences shape learners' internal attributions, observing that the expectations of significant others (teachers, parents, and peers) greatly affect students' learning strategies as well as their progress in language acquisition.

Procedures

RESEARCH QUESTIONS

Similar to Williams and Burden (1999), the present study explores learners' actual thoughts and feelings concerning their own successes and failures in learning a foreign language. Based on previous findings and the theories outlined earlier in this chapter, I asked the following research questions:

1. What do learners mean by succeeding in the foreign language?

2. How can students assess their own development?

3. How do they explain their successes and failures?

4. What actions do they find necessary in order to be more successful learners of English as a foreign language?

5. Are Hungarian students' self-perceptions as language learners similar to those of students in a British context?

PARTICIPANTS AND SETTING

The participants of the study were 30 students learning English in a secondary grammar school in the south of Hungary. The school has a good reputation for its high standard of teaching and is very popular in the region. Although in its newly written educational programme special emphasis is laid on skills development and the necessity of conveying general knowledge, the school is traditionally achievement oriented. The students and teachers are primarily evaluated by examination results, and this practice often causes a rather competitive atmosphere. In spite of the heavy workload, most learners are highly motivated and wish to continue their studies in tertiary education.

Two groups of students were chosen for the current research, all from Year 9 (ages 14–15). As far as the method of subject selection is concerned, a convenience sample was used on the basis of availability and easy accessibility. I taught English to the larger group (16 students), whereas the other learners (14 students) came from a parallel class. The students had similar educational backgrounds, they had all been in the same school for three years, they had five English classes a week, and most of them were at a pre-intermediate level. Both classes were part of the school's 6-year training programme, which means that the students would be at secondary school from 12 until 18 years of age. I selected Year 9 because those students were in the middle of their secondary education, they already had a great deal of experience as language learners, and they were open and mature enough to express their ideas.

DATA COLLECTION METHODS

Three types of data were collected for the purposes of the research, all from the participants' perspectives: interviews, narratives, and feedback from self-assessment. To gather as much information as possible, the students' native language was used throughout the study. Therefore, I translated the samples of responses presented in this chapter.

Interviews

In the first phase, the researchers conducted structured interviews with the learners. Because the questions were an adapted version of the interview schedule used by Williams and Burden (1999), we piloted the interview instrument. To avoid researcher bias, the teacher of the parallel English class was also involved in the investigation. She participated in the validation process and conducted the interviews with my students. The key questions that we asked are listed in the Appendix.

The aim of the pilot stage was to provide clearly worded, unambiguous questions, which conveyed the ideas of the original interview schedule. After translating the questions, we conducted pilot interviews with four students from the same population, Year 9, but from different study groups, to see if the questions elicited meaningful answers. During these sessions, we had to paraphrase and explain some of the items used by Williams and Burden (1999) until we found the most appropriate way of wording the questions. As a result, we changed question 5, "Give me an example of when you did well," into "Give me an example of when you experienced a feeling of success"; and question 9, "Give me an example of when you did not do well," into "Give me an example of when you failed." Similarly, in the case of question 13, we thought that the revised version, "How can you judge how well you are doing?" was more to the point than the original "How can you tell how well you are doing?"

For question 12, we decided to replace the original "What do you have to do to do well in French?" with "What advice would you give someone who wanted to master English?" We made this change because we felt that the question was somewhat vague. We thought that by asking students to give useful advice, we would also ask them to think about what they were actually doing to improve their English. And indeed, already in the pilot stage, participants listed ways in which they were practising the language.

The actual interviews were then carried out in the school library. We made sure that none of the participants were interviewed by their own teacher, because we thought that students might feel more comfortable with a stranger and thus give more truthful answers. The interviewer started each session with an informal discussion about what the students were doing in their English class and how they felt about it. The interviews were recorded and transcribed. They varied in length between 10 and 15 minutes, and because some students were better than others at verbalising their thoughts, they also varied in how informative they were.

Narratives

In the second phase of the data collection, the students wrote about an event in their lives during which they experienced a feeling of success in connection with English. We asked them to recall a particular case and describe what happened and how they felt about it. They wrote their accounts in class, but without writing their names on the papers.

Although question 5 of the interview ("Give me an example of when you experienced a feeling of success") was meant to reveal the same type of information as the student narratives, we requested the narratives because many participants only gave short, superficial answers to question 5. We thought that if students were given more time to think about a successful situation and they were on their own, they would provide more information. In this case as well, however, the accounts varied considerably in length and content. Some participants wrote detailed descriptions of their feelings, and others only listed several occasions without elaborating on them.

Feedback Notes on Self-Assessment

The third type of data consisted of short, written, anonymous feedback, eliciting an even more specific answer. For a period of two weeks, the students were asked to write one sentence on a piece of paper immediately after each English class. They were told to complete either of the following sentences: (1) "I think I did well today, because . . ."; or (2) "I do not think I did very well today, because. . . ." These sentences were then collected and put in an envelope.

DATA ANALYSIS

All the data was analysed using the constant comparative method, as described by Maykut and Morehouse (1994), to find emerging patterns. We determined the initial categories by reviewing the information gathered during the interview sessions. Then, as a result of a thorough analysis of the narratives and the feedback notes, we modified these groupings and constructed new categories.

To enhance the trustworthiness of the research, we used the widely accepted technique of peer debriefing (Maykut & Morehouse, 1994). This technique involved critical analysis of the research method and the data by a fellow researcher, who went through the audit trail and commented on each step. She reviewed the research instruments and checked the information gathered from the students to see if her interpretation of the findings corresponded with my interpretation.

Results

In this section, I present the results along with the corresponding research questions.

1. WHAT DO LEARNERS MEAN BY SUCCEEDING IN THE FOREIGN LANGUAGE?

Table 1 summarises the information gathered from the three data sources. It shows that the participants of this study saw the ability to communicate effectively and to understand what is said as the most important measure of success.

By *communication,* students explained that they meant the ability to talk to native speakers of English and to people from other countries to build relationships. They felt it was important to use the language in real-life situations. For example, students shared the following comments: "When I met foreigners in the summer and I could talk to them, then I felt that yes, I'm doing well. I could make myself understood." "The greatest success is when I can make myself understood by anybody." "It was interesting for me to use my English 'for real' at last." Students also related feelings of success when speaking English with peers in class, as in this response: "When we play games in class . . . we can speak a lot . . . and I always feel good after games."

Comprehension included understanding books, pop songs, films, and television programmes. Responses relating to comprehension included the following: "I saw a film in English and I could understand it quite well. . . . I felt that it was worth learning it." "It felt good when we were watching an English-speaking programme with Dad or Mum, and they asked me to translate it for them if I could. I did so well that even I was surprised." Naturally, comprehension also referred to understanding live English. Many respondents described instances

Table 1. Students' Notions of Success

Item	Frequency
Communicating	58
Comprehension	50
Classroom performance	39
School tests/marks	22
Exams/competitions	21
Accuracy	6

Note: Frequency indicates how often students mentioned the given category in the three stages of data collection.

from summer trips: "I could understand nearly everything the tour guides were saying." "Another good thing about that holiday was that my sister and I interpreted for our parents. . . . I was indispensable." On the other hand, many students mentioned the ability to follow what the teacher or their peers said in class, as reflected in this comment and several other feedback notes: "I think I did well today because I understood everything."

Another major source of success that most learners identified was classroom performance. A large number of responses that fell into this category came from the end-of-class feedback notes, and they referred to (a) the successful performance of a particular task, such as homework or a grammar exercise; (b) the students' creativity, as in writing a dialogue, for example; or (c) their active involvement in class. Answers included the following: "I did well today because I could join in," "I didn't do well today because I wasn't active," and "I didn't do well today because I didn't say a word."

An interesting finding is that good test results and school marks were not mentioned as primary measures of success. Similarly, although passing the state language examination was an obvious goal for many students, there was little mention of it. On the other hand, when asked about a concrete successful event, a few students remembered language competitions that brought them a sense of achievement. The question of accuracy also emerged from responses such as, "I did well today because I didn't make any mistakes," "I think I did well today because I remembered the prepositions," and "I don't think I did very well today because I used the wrong tense in a dialogue."

2. HOW CAN STUDENTS ASSESS THEIR OWN DEVELOPMENT?

Although the responses show a considerable reliance on feedback from the teacher in the form of marks and test results, an internal sense of competence seemed to play the primary role in students' judgments (see Table 2). Understanding and communicating effectively appeared again, as in "If I see a text that we haven't read in the English lesson and I can understand it," "If I can understand things after the first explanation," and "If I don't know a word but I can paraphrase it." Comments such as "If I can do the homework" and "If I can

Table 2. Students' Assessments of Their Performance

Item	Frequency
Sense of competence	26
Feedback from teacher	24
Comparison with others	16
Internal measure	7

do a task easily and quickly" underlined the importance of task performance for the learners.

As shown in Table 2, a large proportion of the participants compared themselves with the others in the group. What is interesting, however, is that many of them had their own internal measures ("I can feel it") and compared their performance to their own abilities. The following comment reveals a mature, highly motivated learner: "I have my own measure . . . so I can decide if I'm at the top of my form or below. . . . I sometimes analyse myself, consider my performance to see how I can improve."

3. HOW DO STUDENTS EXPLAIN THEIR SUCCESSES AND FAILURES?

Table 3 summarises students' perceived reasons for their successes, and Table 4 presents the reasons for failure. Students identified a mixture of external and internal attributes; however, a more thorough analysis reveals that the majority of learners attributed their successes and failures primarily to internal reasons.

As can be seen from the two tables, hard work and concentration emerged as two major factors accounting for success and failure. At the same time, affective

Table 3. Reasons for Success

Item	Frequency
Learning/working hard	32
Attitude/interest/motivation/anxiety	17
Listening and concentrating	14
Practising outside class	14
Teacher	12
Encouragement/help from family and peers	11

Table 4. Reasons for Failure

Item	Frequency
Not working hard enough	33
Language/task difficulty	22
Not listening/concentrating	19
Being tired	13
Bad mood	10
Missing class	8

variables such as attitude, motivational intensity, and anxiety also appeared to be remarkable reasons for success, as the following comments show: "I think it is important to be interested," "It depends on the topic, whether I like it," "It is a question of willpower," "I am responsible for speaking well," and "When I speak English with somebody, I don't feel anxious." Students also mentioned external attributes such as the role of the teacher or the attitudes of others, as reflected in the following comments: "The teacher helped a lot," "It also depends on the teacher . . . her explanations are easy to follow and we can ask a question, and it helps a lot," "My sister helps me," and "We [students] help each other before tests."

Another salient factor which students held responsible for failure was the difficulty of the English language or a particular task. For example, "There are certain grammar points where I don't see the logic . . . we don't have it in Hungarian," "The rules may have been too difficult," and "It happens that I don't understand something." Despite the fact that external factors such as being tired, not being in the mood, or having missed classes were often mentioned, the attributes for failure were internal in most instances, as they were for successes.

4. WHAT ACTIONS DO STUDENTS FIND NECESSARY IN ORDER TO BE MORE SUCCESSFUL LEARNERS OF ENGLISH AS A FOREIGN LANGUAGE?

To answer this question, responses to interview item 12—"What advice would you give someone who wanted to master English?"—were analysed, and the most common ideas are summarised in Table 5.

Obviously, working hard was the most prominent category, but the students went further. Besides the general advice, "You have to learn regularly," they also pinpointed the focus of learning, for example: "If somebody is good at speaking, they should concentrate on grammar, and if somebody is better at grammar, they should practise pronunciation," and "Learning everyday words and dialogues

Table 5. Advice for Mastering English

Item	Frequency
Learn/work hard	33
Practice outside class	31
Ask for help	9
Attitude/motivation	9
Concentration/active involvement in class	5
Go to English-speaking countries	5

is most important." Practising the language outside the English class seemed to be given equal importance, and ideas such as reading books and magazines, watching films and television programmes, and practising speaking were often mentioned. The role of the teacher also emerged in this area: "It is very important to choose a good teacher," "A good teacher is essential," and "If you don't understand something, talk to your teacher about it."

Other responses referring to the value of motivation, active involvement in class, and travelling abroad were also worthy of note: "You must have a goal . . . some motivation, and then everything goes better," "You should be interested in the culture," "First of all you have to like the language," "You should be active in class," and "If you go abroad, you are compelled to speak." Again, as can be seen from the examples, students appear to attribute success to internal rather than external factors.

5. ARE HUNGARIAN STUDENTS' SELF-PERCEPTIONS AS LANGUAGE LEARNERS SIMILAR TO THOSE OF STUDENTS IN A BRITISH CONTEXT?

This last research question can be answered on the basis of the previously discussed findings. It should be mentioned that, although Williams and Burden (1999) investigated different age groups, for comparative purposes here I refer only to the data from the Year 9 students in their study.

When students judged their progress in learning the foreign language, both samples showed a strong reliance on feedback from the teacher. British respondents relied mainly on marks and test results, whereas Hungarian students appeared to give primary importance to self-assessment—that is, an internal sense of understanding and communication.

Learners' perceived reasons for success and failure proved to be very similar. British and Hungarian students alike provided a wide range of attributions, including effort as well as help and encouragement from others. At the same time, two other prominent factors seemed to emerge from the responses of Hungarian students: attitude and extra practice outside class. Similarly, although both groups referred to ability, the notion of language difficulty seemed to be more salient in the Hungarian context.

As regards actions that participants saw as necessary to becoming more successful language learners, strategies such as effort, practice, and revision appeared to figure prominently in both studies. Yet what made the two samples different was the way students determined success. British students listed classroom activities as areas of success and seemed to set performance goals for themselves, whereas Hungarian students placed greater emphasis on extracurricular activities. Furthermore, Hungarian students considered attitude and motivation essential contributors to success, but the British study made no mention of those factors.

Reflection

My aim in this study was to understand my students' views about doing well in learning English, rather than making broad generalisations and drawing far-reaching conclusions. Nevertheless, I am convinced that the outcome may provide useful insight into students' beliefs and expectations, and thus contribute to a better understanding of the workings of the learners' minds.

The data from this study suggest that the respondents enjoyed learning English, and, although most of the time they were satisfied with themselves, they all wished to improve. Their responses revealed a positive attitude towards the English language and the culture studied, and they seemed to recognise their own responsibility for their development. Despite the fact that they mentioned external as well as internal factors as accountable for their successes and failures, in most instances internal reasons were predominant.

The wide range of internal attributions seems to provide evidence of students' developing autonomy and self-awareness. Unlike the British students, the participants of this study appeared to see the foreign language as more important than a school subject, and their aim was to make use of their knowledge and language skills outside the classroom as well. Although they displayed a certain dependence on the teacher, most of them already possessed clearly defined learning goals as well as an internal sense of achievement. Apparently, this finding contradicts the claim that students in an achievement-oriented school mostly set performance goals for themselves. Further observations and a thorough examination of teachers' attitudes and behaviour would be necessary in order to test this hypothesis and draw grounded conclusions.

The most remarkable finding of this study is the differences in how Hungarian and British respondents conceptualised the notion of success. Apparently, for the British students doing well meant performing well in class to get good grades. The Hungarian participants, on the other hand, displayed a certain sense of competence in that they saw success as the ability to communicate effectively and to understand what is said. One possible explanation for this difference was provided by the students themselves. When asked why they wanted to do well in English, many of them gave answers such as "It is important to speak foreign languages today," "So that I can talk to people if I go abroad," "So that I can use it later in my life," "I could use it wherever I travelled," "English is very important in the 21st century," and "English is understood all over the world." If English is today's *lingua franca,* naturally, British students studying another foreign language will not have the same kind of motivation as Hungarian students.

The findings from this study convey a useful message to me as a teacher researcher. Not only do they help me understand my students' needs and ways of thinking, but they also make me reflect on my own teaching practice. I believe that I can contribute to the development of their ability to become successful language learners by building a cooperative classroom atmosphere and creating situations which actively involve them and allow them, in their own words, to "use the language."

Judit Heitzmann teaches at a secondary grammar school in Hungary.

Appendix: Interview Questions

1. Do you like English?

2. What do you like the most? The least?

3. Do you want to do well in English? Why? Why not?

4. How well do you think you are doing?

5. Give me an example of when you experienced a feeling of success.

6. When you do well, what are the main reasons?

7. Is doing well up to you or someone else?

8. Do you ever not do well?

9. Give me an example of when you failed.

10. When you do not do well, what are the main reasons?

11. Is this because of you or someone else?

12. What advice would you give someone who wanted to master English?

13. How can you judge how well you are doing?

CHAPTER 5

The Integration of Literature: A Way to Engage Learners' Intellect and Interest (*Spain*)

Sacramento Jáimez-Muñoz

Issue

For over a decade I have been interested in ways in which literature can be used in the teaching of English with teenagers as a means of stimulating their interest in language learning. The work I report on here reflects my attempt, through an action research project, to implement some of the ideas I have come to embrace over the years. The rationale underlying this work derives mainly from McRae's (1991) idea of literature with a small *l*. This is an integrative view of literature, in contrast to an exclusive view of Literature with a capital *L*, in which only the great works of the cannon are accepted as having literary value. Following Widdowson (1975), McRae considers literature to include all sorts of texts using representational language in a continuum from more to less literary, from proverbs or nursery songs to novels or poems. He has observed that the integration of literature in this broad sense in the language classroom can have a positive effect for the following reason:

> Representational language opens up, calls upon and uses areas of the mind, from imagination to emotion, from pleasure to pain, which referential language does not reach. Where referential language informs, representational language involves. (McRae, 1991, p. 3)

My work is based on the idea that well-selected literary texts, attending to students' interests, offer a variety of relevant materials and activities that can generate a more personal, creative, and autonomous encounter for learners with the foreign language, and that such encounters promote more effective language learning.

The potential offered by literature was particularly appealing in my context, given that my Spanish-speaking students, as speakers of another of the most international languages, did not feel a real need to use much English on a daily basis. I felt that by integrating literature into our work I could give them opportunities to use English not just to learn language but also to read and enjoy interesting texts, which were also instructive from a sociocultural and sociolinguistic point of view. Thus I hoped that working with literature would encourage my learners to discuss and identify with universal attitudes and cultural values most Europeans share: the need of freedom, love, and care; respect for human rights and the environment; and the importance of democratic relationships.

Background Literature

While I carried out the intervention and reflected on the teaching and learning process that it generated, I became more conscious of the complexity of such a process and of the fact that my teaching practice would improve with a better knowledge of the most generally accepted principles of second language acquisition (SLA) research. While reading some basic literature related to SLA (Brown, 1994; Ellis, 1994; Spolsky, 1989; Stern, 1992), I realised that the explanations of the language learning process to a great extent connected with the ideas in a bibliography on using literature in English language teaching (ELT) that I consulted (Brumfit & Carter, 1986; Hill, 1986; Lazar, 1993; McRae, 1991; Maley, 2001). That is, mainstream SLA research seemed to agree with two prevalent ideas promoting the integration of literature in the language classroom:

- The more interested in the topic the students are, the better is their attitude to deal with it and the greater their disposition to make the effort to understand it.

- The richer the variety of language—in this case, texts—the learners are exposed to, and the richer the variety of activities they engage in, the greater the opportunities they have to apply their personal style of learning.

Most of the resource books I consulted for ideas on integrating literature in the syllabus (e.g., Bowler & Parminter, 1993; Collie & Porter-Ladousse,

1991; Collie & Slater, 1998; Duff & Maley, 1990; McRae & Boardman, 1984; McRae, 1992; and Maley, 1994) offered not only an important diversity of texts about themes that can be relevant to teenagers, but also sample tasks that can make those texts accessible to different types of students.

Procedures

Almost a decade after I started to integrate literature in the language classroom, I designed an action research project for a group of students attending post-obligatory secondary education in Spain (known locally as *1° de Bachillerato*). The students were 16 to 17 years old and attended a public high school in Granada. My idea was to observe systematically if a more sustained use of literary texts, selected with attention to students' needs and likes but also to some of the teacher's interests, could really increase their motivation and improve their overall language competence. These are the stages I followed in implementing this action research project:

1. I prepared an initial questionnaire to do a basic needs analysis and to discover students' attitudes toward learning English and the English teacher.

2. I selected the most successful texts and related activities used with similar groups in previous years to start creating what might be called a complementary literary syllabus.

3. I read more resource books, collections of short stories, and poems to select more suitable and relevant literary materials and activities for my learners.

4. I integrated these materials into the general syllabus and tried them with an experimental class while teaching a control group according to the set textbook.

5. I observed how learners interacted with one another and the texts, and I made notes about their difficulties, reactions, and participation.

6. I reflected on the ways the texts and activities I used seemed to shape learners' attitudes and learning.

7. I designed exams, a final questionnaire, and an interview to determine learners' progress, feelings, and opinions about the way we worked and the experience of integrating literature.

8. I analysed the data I collected to evaluate the overall impact of my intervention.

Given my inexperience as a researcher, I was initially uncertain of how to proceed but benefited greatly from the advice and support of an experienced university teacher, Carmen Pérez Basanta, who had worked for many years in secondary education. She guided me to select many useful readings on ELT research and on a language-based approach to literature. Also I felt encouraged by the affirmation of Nunan (1992), who stated that any action research is worthwhile "if it is initiated by a question, is supported by data and interpretation, and it is carried out by a practitioner investigating aspects of his or her own context of situation" (p. 18). In fact, my research was initiated by two basic questions:

1. What could I do to increase teenage students' intrinsic motivation so that they would learn more English?

2. Could they increase their second language (L2) vocabulary and improve their global use of the target language by constant reading and interaction with relevant literary texts?

For this study, I modified the normal syllabus, integrating a variety of literary texts and related tasks according to the themes covered in the textbook used by the learners who participated in this study. The themes were teenage life; science: fact and fiction; music; art and artists; risks, travelling, and adventure; growing up; home and away; science: past, present, and future; natural disasters; the gender gap; money matters; and literature and culture.

During the implementation of the new syllabus, however, not all worked as ideally imagined. I realized that some texts and tasks were more difficult than expected for some students and had to be adapted or replaced with easier ones. Nevertheless, we all learned quite a bit, and I became more aware of two important facts about my learners, which could apply to other learners as well:

1. When learners are interested in the topic, they put forth more effort and can use more related vocabulary words to understand a given text.

2. If the task is challenging enough but not too difficult, learners can access the text better and feel gratified by the challenge.

DETERMINING CONTEXT AND PARTICIPANTS

I asked the principal of my school to assign me to two similar classes (both studying the 1st *Bachillerato*), then I decided which would be the experimental group and which the control group. The syllabus for the experimental group would be enriched with a varied collection of short stories, poems, extracts of novels and plays, proverbs, jokes, limericks, quotations and idioms, and suitable tasks and activities to practise the traditional four skills (listening, reading, speaking, and writing) plus the skills of thinking and imagining or visualizing. The control group would follow the textbook material without any adaptation.

I assigned the groups in such a way as to contribute to the reliability of the investigation. In the first weeks, both classes filled in their student cards (with personal and academic information); answered a questionnaire on attitude, motivation, needs, and teacher characteristics (see Appendix A); and took a diagnostic test covering five aspects of language learning (grammar, vocabulary, writing, listening, and reading). After analysing these collected data, I determined that class 1° B, made up of more boys than girls, with slightly lower motivation and results, would be more suitable as the experimental group. I designated Class 1° A, made up of more girls than boys, slightly more motivated to practise English, and more willing to read, as the control group. My intention was to prevent a common biased tendency: "The difficulty with action research projects of any kind are first that they are often conducted by the innovators themselves, and with experimental groups that beat control groups" (Wragg, 1994, p. 112).

Over a period of 7 months, the control group mainly worked with the textbook and extensively read three graded readers—from pre-intermediate to upper-intermediate—two compulsory and one optional, and an original short story. The experimental group, however, worked with all sorts of literary texts and a wide range of tasks and activities related to them (see Appendix B for sample materials). Members of the experimental group also extensively read seven compulsory original short stories and three optional ones. In the case of the control group, the activities and tasks provided in the textbook were carried out without modification. In the case of the experimental group, all the readings, except the introductory one of every unit, were substituted by literary texts on related topics and their corresponding activities of comprehension, vocabulary, language awareness, and oral and written production.

In explaining my intervention, it is also important to comment on how I selected the texts and how students used them, that is, how classes were organised and what students were required to do in class and at home.

SELECTING LITERARY TEXTS

I believe that choosing suitable literary texts for a given group of students is the single most important issue in the effective integration of literature in the EFL curriculum. My first criterion was to choose texts with themes that were relevant to my students or that told a catching story that would attract their interest and generate personal involvement. Interviewed by Pérez Basanta (1994), McRae said that a text is relevant if it strikes a chord with students. My second criterion was accessibility. This term could be defined as the potential a text has for embodying a common human theme which can be made comprehensible to learners through suitable tasks. I tried to select or design tasks according to the linguistic, cultural, or conceptual difficulty of the text to facilitate the learners' understanding or guide their interaction with it and their partners.

USING LITERARY TEXTS

Experts advise that the second most important step after choosing suitable texts for students is to use them in an appropriate way. My methodological approach to integrating literature in my classes relied on pedagogic principles suggested by McRae (1991) and Carter and McRae (1996) and supported by findings in SLA research:

- **Language-based principle.** The idea is not to teach literature, but to use it as an available resource to teach language.

- **Process-oriented principle.** The literary texts are not seen as complete products to be studied, but as means to stimulate and acquire the processes of reading and writing.

- **Task-based principle.** To ensure learner engagement in class, the teacher has to plan a series of tasks which help students discover and solve problems by themselves and keep them actively involved with the texts and their partners.

- **Student-centred principle.** The relation between the teacher and the class becomes more collaborative and democratic. The teacher usually plans and organizes the work to be done in class beforehand, but once the class starts it is time for students to work. They use the language and interact with the teacher, their classmates, and the texts. The teacher's role is to facilitate student work and to motivate, observe, and cooperate with them. For that reason it is important to capture their interest and increase their participation.

To respect these principles, although with an eclectic attitude, I not only selected relevant materials but also tried to organise classes as Widdowson suggested:

> I think that what one needs to do in thinking how to devise a content for language learning in class is to ask: "Who are these people? . . . What is their background? What are their preoccupations, their assumptions, their beliefs? What is their culture as young people?" (cited in Johns, 1996, p. 39)

IMPLEMENTING A LANGUAGE-BASED LITERARY CLASS FRAMEWORK

Taking into consideration the pedagogical principles I identified, the basic class framework I followed had six steps:

1. **Doing warm-ups.** Oral activities before reading or listening to a literary text tried to capture learners' attention, and activate their schema and their previous language and world knowledge.

2. **Participating in oriented reading or listening.** Reading or listening to the text was done with a given purpose—usually to understand the gist of the text; to confirm or disprove the hypothesis the learner had made about its content, genre, vocabulary, characters, or themes; or to scan for information.

3. **Rereading the text to engage in linguistic or prestylistic activities.** The idea was to do facilitating tasks related to any of the more interesting linguistic features in a given text, such as its lexis, syntax, graphology, phonology, semantics, cohesion, dialect, register, function, or style.

4. **Interacting with the text and classmates.** We carried out a basic analysis of the discourse, how the language functions to create meaning, then exchanged information about the plot, the characters and their relationships, the major themes, the writer's methods, and students' responses.

5. **Postreading and doing wrap-up tasks.** We progressed from less to more open communicative tasks such as role-plays, simulations, discussions about certain aspects or students' interpretations of the text, and projects or creative writing (e.g., writing a different ending or a letter to the author or a given character; creating and describing a new character; creating poems about the topic or with clue words; changing the text from prose to poem, from proverbs to song, from poem to letter, from indirect to direct speech; writing a sketch to be acted out; writing a script for a film from a given short story; or doing the casting).

6. **Completing homework.** Most of the creative writing tasks and the projects had to be revised and finished at home individually, in pairs, or in small groups. I also assigned compulsory or free extensive reading on which the next lesson would be based.

COLLECTING DATA

During the intervention, I used different instruments to obtain a variety of data from the experimental and control groups to see if there were any meaningful differences between them in terms of motivation, perception of the subject and the teacher, and language progress. Seliger and Shohamy (1989) point out that "the use of a variety of methods, irrespectively of underlying assumptions, will lead to a better and more thorough understanding of the topic researched" (p. 257). So to obtain qualitative and quantitative data to be contrasted, I used the following:

• A personalized student card

• An initial questionnaire on motivation and needs

- Two global exams (180 items), consisting of a diagnostic test and a final exam including Schmitt's (2001) vocabulary test of 2,000 words

- Classroom observation

- Portfolios consisting of learners' writings and projects

- An in-depth interview in Spanish (with experimental group members) about the experience

- A final questionnaire on the methodology, the materials, the exams, and the teacher

Results

The qualitative data gathered through the long interview (see Appendix C) showed that most students in the experimental group felt that they had been motivated, worked in a more autonomous way, and acquired more English during the study. The majority of the students answered that they liked most texts they had read and that reading original literary texts had been challenging. They found that the related activities and tasks, particularly the creative ones and discussions, had helped them understand the texts better and use the language to express their own ideas and feelings. Further, they said that this experience, although especially hard at the beginning when working with "Eveline" by James Joyce or "The Black Cat" by Edgar Allan Poe, had undoubtedly been rewarding because they believed they had improved their use of English, particularly their reading skills and vocabulary. Some learners even felt that this experience had been worthy in a more global personal and cultural sense. Here are examples of their comments on the value of the experience:

- "Of course, I have learnt English in general. . . . Now speaking a lot of vocabulary; and with the texts, more vocabulary, I had very little [vocabulary previously]—the verbs, the structures, too."

- "It helps you to learn culture and a lot of new vocabulary. . . . Although you are not conscious of many words that are in the texts, later you recognise them when you encounter them again."

- "I notice a great improvement, and not only in English, also in other things. . . . even in reading Spanish, you understand things better."

- "It also helps you to know about what life is. You don't just deal with English."

These data coincided with those obtained through the final questionnaire (see Appendix D), which was completed by the control group and the experimental group and was anonymous; they had to indicate only if they belonged to Group A or B. This instrument addressed two very important aspects of the study: (1) if, when answering anonymously, the experimental learners would evaluate the experience as positively as they did in the face-to-face interview, and (2) whether the control learners had perceived any lack of demand, dedication, or enthusiasm on my part, as the teacher. In relation to this latter point, I thought it was especially necessary to have some evidence that I did not act significantly differently in each group, biasing the investigation in favour of the experimental one.

With respect to the first of these two issues, the fourth item in Section 1 of the final questionnaire asked learners about how their learning was affected by reading and doing tasks with original literary texts. (The control group, which followed the set textbook, also did some limited work with literary texts during the year.) Table 1 summarizes the responses of the experimental and control groups; it shows clearly that the views of the experimental group were much more positive.

The issue of the teacher's attitude was addressed in Section 3 of the final questionnaire, which consisted of the same list of qualities of a good teacher as in the initial questionnaire. For most items, both groups evaluated the teacher in a very similar way. For example, learners' evaluations of "The teacher is demanding,

Table 1. Learners' Evaluations of the Impact of Working With Original Literary Texts

Group	Response	Frequency	Percentage
Control	Nothing	2	7.7
	A bit	7	26.9
	Quite much	14	53.8
	Very much	3	11.5
	Total	26	100.0
Experimental	Nothing	0	0
	A bit	2	7.7
	Quite much	6	23.1
	Very much	18	69.2
	Total	26	100.0

Note: Control percentages do not equal 100 because of rounding.

but fair" are shown in Table 2, and Table 3 shows their evaluations of "The teacher transmits enthusiasm."

There was an important difference of opinion, however, with respect to the promotion of autonomy. As Table 4 shows, the experimental group felt more strongly that the teacher promoted autonomy, which might suggest that integrating literature in the language classroom facilitated more autonomous learning.

Table 2. Learners' Views on Extent to Which Teacher Was Demanding but Fair

Group	Response	Frequency	Percentage
Control	Nothing	0	0
	A bit	0	0
	Quite much	6	23.1
	Very much	20	76.9
	Total	26	100.0
Experimental	Nothing	0	0
	A bit	0	0
	Quite much	4	15.4
	Very much	22	84.6
	Total	26	100.0

Table 3. Learners' Views on Extent to Which Teacher Transmitted Enthusiasm

Group	Response	Frequency	Percentage
Control	Nothing	0	0
	A bit	0	0
	Quite much	6	23.1
	Very much	20	76.9
	Total	26	100.0
Experimental	Nothing	0	0
	A bit	0	0
	Quite much	5	19.2
	Very much	21	80.8
	Total	26	100.0

Table 4. Learners' Views on Extent to Which Teacher Promoted Learner Autonomy

Group	Response	Frequency	Percentage
Control	Nothing	0	0
	A bit	3	11.5
	Quite much	13	50.0
	Very much	10	38.5
	Total	26	100.0
Experimental	Nothing	0	0
	A bit	0	0
	Quite much	6	23.1
	Very much	20	76.9
	Total	26	100.0

In relation to the quantitative data obtained with the initial and final tests, Figures 1 and 2 show that the intervention adopted to improve the learners' global use of language had positive results. The experimental students improved their reading, writing, listening, grammar, and vocabulary more than the students in the control group, who started from a slightly better position (and actually dropped a bit in reading).

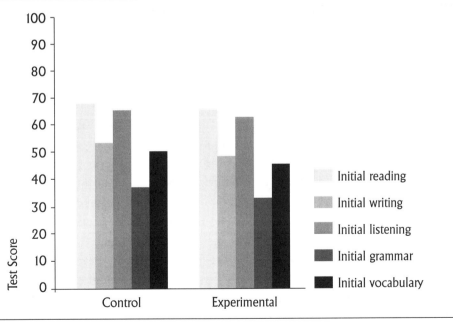

Figure 1. Results of the initial test.

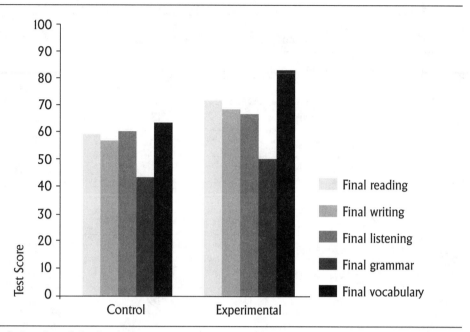

Figure 2. Results of the final test.

As I explained earlier, the pretest and posttest each consisted of five parts: reading, writing, listening, grammar, and vocabulary. The results of the experimental group's final tests were better than those of the control group in general terms, which might be due not only to the intervention but to other factors or forms of learning, even outside school. Nevertheless, I think that it is reasonable to claim that the intervention did play a role in the improvements in learning achieved by the experimental group.

Reflection

The results of this action research project provided insight about the learners as well as my role as teacher. At the learners' level, the generally positive feedback of the experimental students indicates that integrating literary texts that tell a good story or are relevant and challenging for students can increase the learners' motivation to use, manipulate, or play with the target language. As a result, this strategy can enhance their comprehension of how the language works and their interest in the process of learning it.

For me, as the teacher, doing action research—including the unavoidable difficulties and pitfalls—has been very rewarding in terms of enhancing an awareness of my personal teaching practice and of my students' learning. Also, through this reflective process of inquiry I became more confident in the potential that action research offers a teacher for understanding the teaching and learning process from the perspectives of teachers and learners.

At a more practical level, I have found evidence that the use of well-chosen literary texts offers learners many opportunities to practise English, to gain cultural awareness about English-speaking societies, and to gain cross-cultural awareness about universal feelings and values. Consequently, I have integrated literature in my syllabus as a central resource not only for postobligatory secondary education, but also for lower levels.

Finally, the work I have conducted is also worthwhile given the lack of research into how teachers of English use literature and incorporate it into their work, as well as the lack of research into the effects such measures have on learners and learning. The work I have presented here makes a small contribution to this area of research, one which I hope will provide guidance and ideas for practitioners who wish to use literature in their work as well as to study the impact it has on learners.

Sacramento Jáimez-Muñoz teaches at
Francisco Ayala secondary school in Granada, Spain.

Appendix A: Initial Questionnaire on Attitude, Motivation, Needs, and the Teacher

Read each question and answer it carefully or circle the number you give it. Please, take it seriously as your teacher needs to know your initial attitude and expectations about the teacher and this subject.

0 = nothing, 1= a bit, 2 = quite much, and 3 = very much

Circle your group: 1° A / 1° B

1. Do you think learning English is necessary?   0   1   2   3

2. Do you really like learning English?   0   1   2   3

3. How important is English in relation to the other subjects?   0   1   2   3

4. Choose the three most necessary skills to learn English among the ones below:
   —Speaking
   —Listening
   —Using the dictionary
   —Writing
   —Reflecting about grammar

—Translating
—Reading

5. Choose the three most important activities to improve your competences:
   —Compositions
   —Conversation
   —Language functions practice
   —Doing projects
   —Reading
   —Learning strategies training
   —Working with video
   —Word work
   —Pronunciation practice
   —Grammar work
   —Culture awareness

6. Choose the three factors that you think can favour your learning more:
   —The teacher's attitude
   —Classroom syllabus
   —Speaking English
   —The textbook and workbook
   —Your attitude and interest
   —Your family's support
   —Class timetable
   —Your classmates' attitude

7. Choose the three most important characteristics of a good English teacher:
   —She should be demanding but fair.
   —She should transmit enthusiasm.
   —She should have a good level of English.
   —She should be kind and friendly.
   —She should keep the discipline and have a good classroom management.
   —She should prepare and organize classes well.
   —She should be receptive and be always ready to help.
   —She should offer a variety of activities.
   —She should create a good working atmosphere.
   —She should explain things clearly.
   —She should promote learners' autonomy.
   —She should have a good knowledge of the subject.
   —She should treat her students with respect.
   —She should assess students' work and progress fairly.

Appendix B: Sample From a Unit Integrating Language and Literature

One of the most relevant themes for our teenage students is music. This is part of the unit designed to help them read and enjoy learning English through music.

UNIT: MUSIC AND SOUND

Contents

b) **Intensive reading**
- · A poem: "I Hear America Singing" by Walt Whitman
- · Songs: "So Young" by the Corrs, and learners' favourite English songs to be compared, analysed, and used to create their own song
- · Some proverbs related to music
- · A haiku

c) **Extensive reading**
A short story: "Hannah" by Malachi Whitaker (extensive reading in class)

Task 1: A Poem: "I Hear America Singing" by Walt Whitman

Listen and while you read the poem, circle the words related to sound and underline the jobs mentioned.

I hear America singing, the varied carols I hear,

Those of mechanics, each one singing his as it should be, blithe and strong,

The carpenter singing his as he measures his plank or beam,

The mason singing his as he makes ready for work, or leaves off work,

The boatman singing what belongs to him in his boat, the deckhand singing on the steamboat deck.

The shoemaker singing as he sits on his bench, the hatter singing as he stands,

The wood-cutter's song, the ploughboy's on his way in the morning, or at the noon intermission or at sundown;

The delicious singing of the mother, or of the young wife at work, or of the girl sewing or washing,

Each singing what belongs to her, and to none else;

The day what belongs to the day—at night, the party of young fellows, robust, friendly,

Singing with open mouths their strong melodious songs.

- **Personal reaction**

   Do you like this poem? Why?

   What is special about its lines?

- **Linguistic and prestylistic analysis**

   ➢ **Lexis**

   Classify the words found in the corresponding column.

Sound & Music	Country Jobs	Town Jobs	Sea Jobs

   ➢ **Grammar**

   What is special about its structure?

   How many complete sentences is this poem made of?

   What tense is it written?

   Why is the form –ing used all through it?

   Why do you think the poet has used it? What image does it offer you?

   ➢ **Period**

   Is it a poem about nowadays or about some time past?

   What words or lines can help you to decide?

   ➢ **Cohesion**

   What do these pronouns refer to?

   "each" and "his" in line 2

   "him" in line 5

   "her" in line 9

   In line 3 there are two "his," are they the same?

- **Discussion**

   How does W. Whitman represent America at the ending of the XIX century? What about women? What role do they play then?

- **Creative writing** (in pairs)

  Write three more lines to add to the poem, but as if it were about the current society. One of them at least about women.

- **Writing a biography**

  Using the information below, write a brief biography of the great American poet Walt Whitman.

—Year of birth: 1819   —Year of death: 1892
—Place of birth: West Hills (Long Island)
—Father: a radical-minded carpenter   —Mother: a Dutch Quaker
—Occupation: working from very young: errand-boy, clerk, printer, teacher in schools in the country
—1831: Whitman became an apprentice on the paper the Long Island *Patriot*
—1846: editor of *The Brooklyn Eagle*   —Partner: W. C. Bryant of *The Evening Post*
—Civil war: nurse to the Union wounded at the battlefields.
—Poems from that time: *The Wounded, Hymn of Dead Soldiers*
—After the war: a clerk in the Department of the Interior in Washington; diminished years later for his work *Leaves of Grass* (considered "indecent")
—1873: moving to Camden (New Jersey); living in poverty most time
—Best work: *Leaves of Grass* (1st published 1855)

Task 2: Proverbs

"The girl who can't dance says the band can't play."

"The older the fiddle the sweeter the tune."

"As the old cock crows, the young cock learns."

- Translate these proverbs into Spanish. Do we have similar ones?

- These proverbs are related to music and sound. The second one uses a common comparative structure. Try to paraphrase the second one, using two different instruments and adjectives, e.g., the thinner the flute, the higher the tune.

Appendix C: The Interview

1. How do you usually feel in the English class?

2. Do you like your textbook this year? Why?

3. Do you like the reading and activities of the book and workbook?

4. Do you like the original literary text you are reading this year?

5. What do you think about the experience of reading original texts?

6. Which ones do you find more difficult? Why do you think it may be so?

7. What do you do to understand these texts better?

8. What do you think of the activities and tasks related to them?

9. Are the topics of these texts relevant to you?

10. Do you think that if you are interested in the topic you can understand the text better? Why may it be so?'

11. What do you find most and least interesting about English class this year?

12. Do you do all the extensive readings I assigned for homework?

13. Can this reading of original literary text help you to learn English?

14. Have you really noticed any improvement? In which aspects?

15. Have you learnt something about English culture reading these texts?

16. Do you like reading in Spanish? What do you usually read?

17. Did your parents read you tales when you were a child?

18. Do you usually read during the course? And on holidays?

19. What do you usually read? Why?

20. Do your parents usually read? What do they read?

21. Which ones of the texts we have read have you liked most?

22. Which ones have you not liked?

23. In which aspects are English classes different this year?

24. Do you think it is too much effort reading original texts this year? Is that a challenge or a difficulty?

25. Can this experience be positive for your learning in any respect? In which respect? Explain to me, please.

Appendix D: Final Questionnaire on the Methodology, the Exams, and the Teacher

Please, answer this questionnaire anonymously and honestly so your teacher will be able to know how you evaluate her teaching and your learning this course, which is about to finish. Each section includes several aspects you have to assess from 0 to 3: 0 = nothing, 1 = a bit, 2 = quite much, and 3 = very much.

Circle your group: 1° A / 1° B

Section 1. Evaluation of the methodology:

How important have been the following activities in your learning of English this year?

Speaking English in class whenever you have had the opportunity to do it ......

Listening to the teacher or your mates speaking English ......

Using the textbook and workbook ......

Reading and doing tasks with original literary texts ......

Reading and doing tasks with adapted literary texts (graded readers) ......

The type and variety of the exams ......

Reading extensively ......

Section 2. Evaluation of the exams:

I consider the exams in general have been

a) fair (exams evaluate everything worked in class)

b) valid (each test has evaluated what it intends: written comprehension, grammar, etc.)

c) suitable to the level I study (1° Bachillerato)

In general,

d) I have liked their variety

e) they have helped me learn English in a more global way

f) they measure my level of English in a more global way

Section 3. Evaluation of the teacher:

She's demanding but fair.

She transmits enthusiasm.

She's got a good level of English.

She's kind and friendly.

She keeps the discipline and has a good classroom management.

She prepares and organizes classes well.

She's receptive and is always ready to help.

She offers a variety of activities.

She creates a good working atmosphere.

She explains things clearly.

She promotes learners' autonomy.

She's got a good knowledge of the subject.

She treats her students with respect.

She marks things fairly.

Section 4. Please, add any personal comment on your English classes or teacher this year you think can be useful to improve my didactic practice.

CHAPTER 6

Teachers Into Researchers: Learning to Research in TESOL (*UK*)

Richard Kiely

Issue

There are many perspectives on the purpose of teacher research. It can benefit teachers by providing opportunities to indulge their curiosity, sustain motivation, and further career development. For students it can enhance learning through reflection and self-knowledge. And for the universities, colleges, and language schools hosting the programme being researched, teacher research can enhance reputation through perceptions of client responsiveness and fitness for the purpose of the programme.

The benefits for the wider community are equally important. The origins of action research lie in the need to better understand what effective practice involves in a given context. Kurt Lewin, a key initiator of practitioner research in U.S. industrial contexts in the 1940s, wanted to discover more effective and efficient modes of operation in a steel mill, and his findings could be applied elsewhere. His approach (set out in Lewin, 1946b) established the value of practitioner expertise and insight which could be harnessed to improve practice. This goal is also relevant in education. Educators can learn much from close scrutiny of practice in programmes other than their own: They can gather ideas for materials and assessment formats by analysing a work plan; understand something of the participation and learning experience of students by observing classrooms and other learning processes; and reflect on the effectiveness of teaching strategies by reviewing evidence of learning outcomes.

The topic of this chapter is a context for my own learning at all these levels. Many teacher education programmes have research methods as a core component, and I am familiar with the strands of rationale which derive from the traditions and conventions of master's study in British (and indeed, many other) higher education programmes. While doing programme design and quality assurance for such programmes, I have had many opportunities to explore the strategies and resources used to support learning in research methods. As a coteacher of research methods courses and as an advisor of students doing first degree and graduate research projects, I have seen something of the learning experience. As an assessor and external examiner, I have seen learning outcomes such as essays on research theory, research designs, and dissertations reporting empirical research studies. These experiences have provided ideas for my own teaching and an awareness of the need for a more systematic look at the issues in teaching and learning research methods.

This chapter describes my learning about my students' experiences while they learned to do research in TESOL during a postgraduate master's programme at a British university. I focus on how the research shaped and is continuing to shape my approach to teaching research methods. The process for me has been one of understanding at a deeper level the challenge involved in learning research methods. Thus, it involves a rediscovering of this construct, such that the process of designing and implementing a programme could be viewed from a new perspective each year rather than delivered as a preformed package. The collaborative nature of the programme adds another dimension to the learning, because my evolving approach has to be shared with other tutors and the students on the course. This chapter includes evaluation and research dimensions: I examine the effectiveness of our plans and practices, and I explore the nature and stages of learning to do research on the teaching of English to speakers of other languages.

Background Literature

In terms of the literature, first I looked at rationales for the inclusion of research training in teacher education. Buchberger and Byrne (1995), in a review of teacher education curricula across Europe, called for greater attention to research training in the initial education of teachers. They concluded that "Initial Teacher Education (ITE) as well as INSET [in-service teacher education] will have to find a clear profile for educational research and development and an active involvement of teachers in this" (p. 16). Second, in the UK higher education (HE) sector the centrality of research is a key feature of master's level study.

In a report on postgraduate programmes, Harris (1996) noted that master's programmes "involve a substantial element of research training and/or an element of personal research" (p. 3). Third, a range of research methods handbooks specifically for the TESOL field have attested to the value of such research activity and the particular challenges of equipping teachers with the necessary research skills (e.g., Beaumont & O'Brien, 2000; McDonough & McDonough, 1997; Nunan, 1992; Wallace, 1998).

Empirical studies on teachers and other students learning to research have reported on the challenges faced (e.g., Benson & Blackman, 2003). Deem and Lucas (2002) commented on the dearth of research into the teaching of research methods at the master's level and the need (which they address) to understand the role of research learning in these courses, which are between initial studies in education and doctoral study. Zeuli (1994), investigating how teachers read research, noted that "teachers are interested in knowing specifically the type of learning and teaching focussed on in a classroom research study" (p. 54), and they value credible, concrete case studies. His conclusion suggests that teachers reading research take points of professional relevance from the experience and avoid engaging with theoretical and methodological perspectives.

This observation underlines the need for a training programme in research methods which is not for gleaning new, effective teaching strategies. Cumming, Shi, and So (1997) and Birbili (2003), studying longer doctoral programmes, found that such learning was a gradual process and was linked to engagement with practical aspects of the research task. Their findings have a special relevance for the achievement of learning objectives in 12-month full-time programmes, as studied here. Birbili noted the success of learning rather than teaching, citing Leonard's view that research methods are caught by experience rather than taught by teachers. These analyses by Birbili and Cumming et al. called for innovation and further research into this area:

> Perhaps the most important observation about research training that comes from the literature is that there is a pressing need for all those involved in it to reflect on their current practices and introduce greater flexibility in its organisation and provision. (Birbili, 2003, Conclusion)

> The processes of learning to do research in second language education need to be articulated more precisely than has previously been the case, and such processes made the object of critical enquiry. (Cumming et al., 1997, pp. 431–432)

My study accepts a key assumption in the literature—that research methods training is a relevant, necessary, but challenging dimension of language teacher education—and describes the experience of using a particular teaching strategy to realise this goal.

Procedures

THE RESEARCH CONTEXT

The context for this study is the teaching of a research methods course on a British university's TESOL master's programme. The students on this programme were from a range of international TESOL contexts. The approach to teaching research methods on this course has evolved over many years of stocktaking, self-evaluation, and problem solving by the tutor teams. This approach is set out in Table 1 in three successive phases. Phase 3 is the approach to teaching research methods which the tutors currently use on our master's programme. This approach has three elements:

1. A broad-based introduction to research methods in TESOL and language education

2. A focused critique of one published research report, followed by an oral presentation to peers on the research strategy developed in this report

3. Participation in a series of about 20 oral presentations of research study critiques (approximately 20)

Table 1. Three Phases in the Development of the Programme

Phase	Key Features of the Curriculum
1. Theory to practice	• Input on theories of educational research • Assessment by essay on research theory • In dissertation, students apply this theory *Key problem:* • Serious difficulties experienced at the dissertation stage
2. Practice with a focus on research design	• Input on research practice in TESOL/applied linguistics • Assessment by design of research study • In dissertation, students implement this design *Key problem:* • Research designs insufficiently informed by research practice in TESOL fields
3. Practice with a focus on critique	• Input on research practice in TESOL/applied linguistics • Assessment by critique of a selected research study in TESOL (from a list of 70 studies) • Dissertation informed by generic principles from input, by the detail of the research study critiqued, and through oral presentations, the exposure to the range of articles critiqued

Four factors serve to link these elements of the learning experience:

1. The critique assessment has a washback effect on the course: tutors integrate issues in reading and critiquing research into their sessions, for example, discussing explicitly how practice relating to data analysis or ethics might be critiqued.

2. Throughout the course there is discussion of the nature of the critique the students must do—in particular of the issues which the written critique will cover.

3. The written critique and the tutor feedback on it shape the oral presentation. Students use the feedback (some explicitly referring to the contribution of the tutor) to improve the oral presentation version of the critique.

4. The management of the oral presentation sessions provides a context to revisit the content and topics of the programme as taught. For example, a research study based on interview data provides a context to address generic issues relating to interviews and discuss in a situated way the construct validity and analysis issues.

The study I report on here, then, is an evaluation of a specific course as well as a form of intervention-based research. I was interested in understanding the extent to which the course led to the desired outcomes as well as the way in which tutors' interventions, in structuring the course the way we did, affected students' experiences of learning to do research. Because of the collaborative nature of the work and the data involved, the other tutors contributed to the research presented in this study.

DATA COLLECTION AND ANALYSIS

The approach to data collection in this study had three central features: (1) use of existing data gathered through routine course evaluations, which provided an overview of the research methods course experience; (2) a focus on the personal narrative of students learning to research through the critique and oral presentation experience; (3) a longitudinal dimension, capturing key aspects of students' experiences while learning to research in the 8-month period between writing the critique and completing the dissertation.

Existing Data

I reviewed the results from two questionnaires, which captured student feedback on (1) the input sessions, and (2) the series of oral presentation seminars. Students completed these questionnaires, which are used on all courses in the department, in the last session of each course.

Student Narratives

These data were captured using two specially designed questionnaires and interviews with volunteer students—19 students out of 40 responded to an e-mail request to participate in the interview stage of data collection. The questionnaires were designed to provide (a) an account of previous research experience completed at the start of the programme, and (b) an account of the critique-writing process. The interviews were carried out at the time of oral presentations, and they elicited students' accounts of preparing written critiques and oral presentations. My colleagues and I transcribed all the interviews,[1] then each tutor conducted a content analysis, and the tutors compared their analyses in two workshops. The first workshop explored themes in the interview data, and participants identified categories for further analysis. In the second workshop, participants explored patterns in the data within these categories and related these to patterns in the questionnaire data.

Dissertation Trail

A central aim of the research methods course is to facilitate the completion of a dissertation in TESOL/applied linguistics, a required element of this master's programme. Scrutiny of how students fared in this task was therefore considered an essential part of this research study. If the programme for teaching research methods was successful, then it would have some impact on the process and quality of the dissertation. Therefore, my strategy was to examine the dissertations of the students who were interviewed to identify links between these dissertations and the studies critiqued. Examples of these trails are given in the next section.

Results

This section first presents the findings related to a range of organizational issues. These correspond to the programme structure and have contributed and are still contributing to the development of teaching arrangements. In many ways this discussion reflects the programme evaluation dimension of the study. Second, the findings relating to the learning experience, in particular to the development of a researcher identity, are presented. This discussion affords insights into the process of merging teacher and researcher identities.

PROGRAMME ORGANISATION ISSUES

The innovative features of the programme structure were the outcome of a series of changes to accommodate student needs and learning outcomes. The input–critique–oral presentation structure was designed to marry the broad coverage of research traditions and strategies which might be needed for the completion of an empirical dissertation study with the focused practical research skills which facilitate learning and a sense of readiness for doing research. Feedback from the course evaluation questionnaire attests to success in this respect. The overall satisfaction with the unit achieved a mean of 4.13 (on a 1–5 rating instrument), the highest overall rating of a course evaluated by that group. The mean rating for successful achievement of learning objectives was 3.68, also higher than that of other courses. This is a particularly significant finding given the reputation for difficulty which the research methods course has had.

Results from the course evaluation questionnaire, which students completed after the oral presentation series, also support the value of the structure. Students gave particularly high ratings for how well the course helped them understand the process of developing an oral presentation from a written critique (4.27) and for how well tutor feedback contributed to this process (4.42). Students also valued the tutorials with tutors, when preparing the written critique and developing a presentation from the critique. Petra[2] described in an interview how the discussion with her tutor helped clarify her thinking and understanding of the research study:

> During the tutorial time I think [the tutor] asked me some questions and I found I couldn't answer. But it's a good thing for me because I realised that what was asked will be the main point of my assignment.

Complementing these overall positive perspectives on the programme structure are a range of views on the sequencing of learning activities such as input sessions, assessments, and presentations. Hana articulated the benefits of each student critiquing a different study and then presenting the critique to the whole group:

> Although it is the only one [article] for each of us, we can follow the procedure and look at it very closely and really learn some experience. To look at it critically, to find the strength and weakness of other people's research, and after that when we attend the presentations of our classmates we know more about other researchers; it actually enlarges, broadens our horizons. We know: Oh, there could be that kind of research, research can be like that. So for me after the critique, I know better.

Rudi also commented positively on the benefits of the critique writing:

> Before that [writing the critique] I didn't have any idea about the research methods although I took part in the seminars. It's maybe because I didn't pay much attention on that. And after this critique I did learn a lot, yeah.

In a later interview Rudi summed up the curricular experience in terms which mirrored our rationale:

If I could use a metaphor, I think it's more like a funnel, more from the general into the specific—from the general research programme into the specific research [study].

The dissertation trail element of the study provides data illustrating the quality of Rudi's learning, as shown in Table 2. In Table 2 (and in Table 3), the topic trail considers the relationship between the topic of the article on which a student chose to base his or her critique and presentation, and the topic of the student's dissertation. In this case, "similar" means the two topics were closely related. The methods trail performs the same kind of comparison except that it examines the research methods used in the study critiqued and the student's dissertation. Again, in Rudi's case, the two were very closely related.

In summary, Rudi felt he knew little about research methods to start with (his undergraduate studies were in a humanities programme in English language and literature, and his teacher education studies did not have a systematic element on research in education or the social sciences). The input sessions alone did not support learning, but in combination with the critique activity they afforded a learning experience which resulted in an excellent dissertation.

In cases like Rudi's, a key element of success was the specific guidelines set out for the critique assignment. These were organised to provide a brief list of required elements:

• Introduction to the topic and context of the study

• Descriptive account of the research

• Evaluative commentary on the research

This was followed by a list of 15 questions and cues which students might address. Rita articulated a view held by many of the students interviewed on how these guidelines were a starting point and source of comfort:

> The question as it's set out in the [assignment] handbook is quite helpful because it gives a far more detailed breakdown in this assignment question than the other assignment questions.

Table 2. Data on Critique-Dissertation Links—Rudi

Student	Critique Grade	Dissertation Grade	Topic Trail	Methods Trail
Rudi	A	A	Similarities: *metacognitive strategies* in *listening comprehension*	Similarities: use of *diary studies* with improved data analysis techniques

Rory illustrated clearly the range of resources available by the oral presentation stage and the rich synthesising involved in preparing her presentation:

And before my presentation I take this feedback [on the written critique], discuss with my classmates—I try to integrate my tutor's opinion, so I discuss this feedback with my classmates.

Cleo, in discussing her concerns when preparing her presentation, went beyond mastery of the content of the study. She focused on effective communication and on the challenge of generating a genuine learning experience for other students. This reflects not only the success of the structuring of the learning, but also a key aspect of the research process—effective communication and dissemination.

When I was sitting in my room and I would think about things how can . . . you know, to some students the concepts in this research are difficult to understand, so I would think about how can I begin it and how can I make sure that they understand the research. . . . So I would try to think about the way how to, you know, introduce this research easily, and make it attractive to the other listeners.

These strands in the findings on the organisational aspects of the programme attest to the suitability and effectiveness of the procedures set in place. Students found the specific guidelines and the revisiting elements particularly effective. The guidelines structured the critique-writing process without seriously reducing interpretation and ownership aspects of the task. The revisiting involved serial engagement with the research article, the critique, and tutor feedback in the social context of preparing an oral presentation for an audience of peers.

ISSUES RELATED TO LEARNING IN RESEARCH

The questionnaire results indicate that students overall found that this programme improved their learning about research. The quality of the critique assignments submitted and of the dissertations completed at the end of the course further supports this conclusion. The interview data afford additional insights, which relate to the role of teacher identity in this learning and the development of a researcher perspective which could lead to enhanced teaching skills and research career opportunities.

Students started out by selecting a specific article to critique, and for many students the choice reflected their interest in a particular aspect of professional experience. Rachel and Petra set out the reasons for choosing their articles, and in many ways they reflected the conclusion of Zeuli (1994) that teachers look at research papers for solutions to practical problems.

My topic is about group activity, and when I was teaching in [country] usually I divided students into groups and it was a problem. . . . I'm quite interested and I am seeking some way to improve it. I'm really interested in it, so that's [why] I want to choose the topic. (Rachel)

The article is, as I said in the presentation, is about task repetition. Because this I usually did with my learners, so I think there must be something new. So I want to find out the new ideas for my future teaching. (Petra)

Pam chose an article on teaching grammar because this was an area in which she had a curriculum responsibility in her school. The critique process led her to engage with different ways of understanding effectiveness in grammar teaching:

My area is grammar teaching. . . . And now I will try to think, okay, the opinion from students. . . . Before I just pay attention to the student's opinion; I haven't thought about what teachers think about this task. And now I try to think about the two aspects.

The dissertation trail data on Pam (see Table 3) illustrates the learning value of her reflections. She drew together a professional issue, a perspective in a research article identified as an opportunity during interaction with her critique tutor, and realised this opportunity in her own research to produce an excellent dissertation.

For many students, learning meant a new perspective on their teaching. Hana described how research skills could help her develop her practice as a teacher:

I think I will be more observant, and will be more confident. I think I will, when I go back to my job again, I will notice: Oh this is a researchable area. I will notice that. When I look back I find there were many chances, I could have carried out some research, but I didn't see them. But I now think I will notice; I will realise there were some aspects to explore into.

In addition to teaching-related learning, many students explained how the critique developed their capacity to read research with a more critical eye.

Table 3. Data on Critique-Dissertation Links—Pam

Student	Critique Grade	Dissertation Grade	Topic Trail	Methods Trail
Pam	B	A	Similarities: discussion of *grammar* in *language tests* in critique and in *TESOL pedagogy* in dissertation	Similarities: reliance on data from expert stakeholders (assessors in critique article; teachers in dissertation)

Rana explained how learning to critique was at the heart of her learning to do research:

> When you know how to critique a study then you know where the problem is and you can also know how to research. . . . If you don't have such critiquing skill you just accept everything you read. Maybe there is some problem but you cannot judge it. But if you have critiquing skills it helps you to judge what's right and what's wrong rather than just accept all of them.

The critique task also supported learning by providing a model. Rory noted how doing the critique clarified the structure of students' dissertations, even though they had not decided on a topic or specific issue:

> I think there is a clear picture about the organisation of my dissertation in my mind when I read this research. Maybe the scale of my dissertation is larger than [author of research paper's] research, but I know the organisation very well. And I think that [is] the most clear idea I've got from this assignment.

These comments are particularly revealing, because the analysis of Rory's critique to dissertation trail (as in Tables 2 and 3) did not reveal either topic or methodological similarities. Therefore, what may be articulated here is a connection at a more abstract level, a sense of what research is—its organisation in conceptual and data terms. Students recognised that such scoping or envisioning prior to elaborating a detailed research proposal was a key stage to work through. Some 8 months after this interview, Rory noted the following in an evaluation comment on the dissertation-writing process:

> I would like to say that the [critique] assignment of the Research Methods Course gave me some ideas about my dissertation, because the assignment gave me an opportunity to analyse a piece of research so closely. So, when I was writing my dissertation, I copied some ways the author conducted the research (the targeted research in my assignment), such as the ways he analysed the data, and the ways he organized the whole research, and the logical ways he built his conceptual framework.

Additionally, the critique task constituted opportunities for learning by highlighting deficits in specialist or technical knowledge. Hilda, for example, commented on the challenge of reading sections of papers which used statistics:

> I'm really bad at mathematics, so when all the time anything related to maths I will feel anxious about that. Especially for that quantitative analysis, quantitative research.

Some students also signalled how the critique task had presented a fundamental challenge to their thinking and assumptions. Grace illustrated a capacity for analysis and explanation as she related the argument in the article critiqued (about the passivity of Asian English language learners) to her own experience:

> When I read the article I'm a little bit surprised to find that in fact Asian students don't have a different kind of learning attitude. In their mind they don't have different attitudes, but they still behave differently. So I think, if Asian teachers want to use Western pedagogy they have to work very hard because it's very difficult to persuade their students to participate so actively as European students. But I think at least they [authors of the research article] found that they are not different in their mind, the difference is because of educational system and the culture and traditions.

Grace articulated a major readjustment in her thinking. She drew the conclusion that the classroom behaviours of Asian learners were shaped by "culture and traditions" rather than by their biology; that they are determined by nurture, not nature.

In what may be further evidence of learning to do research, many students came to identify with the role of researcher. Some, like Cara and Rudi, came to share perspective and motivation with the researcher from their own experience:

> Now I realise, inside this article, I have a lot of . . . same experience. (Cara)

> I guess I tried to get into [author of research paper's] work to see the things she sees in her own way, because that way I can explain the whole context. I try not to be outside of that research, I try to get into her work to see why she wants to do that, why she chose that method. And that helped me a lot to understand her motivation. (Rudi)

Robbie expressed his emerging researcher identity in a different manner. He saw in the research study the analysis of a phenomenon familiar to him:

> And yes, I mean mother tongue use is something that's happened in my class-room literally I'm sure, hundreds and hundreds of times. And as [author of research paper] argued in the article, it's a bit blind really to just accept the orthodox view that "English use—good, mother tongue use—bad."

The view here is the researcher as the critical voice, challenging orthodoxies by analysing routine behaviours from a novel perspective and establishing new connections which bring concepts from applied linguistics (in this case, code switching) to the task of understanding what happens in the TESOL classroom.

Reflection

This teacher research study had two significant outcomes, one relating to the organizational issues, and the other to the learning construct. The latter pertains to something both more general and more personal. It is general in the sense that it deals with stages of learning, from initial grappling with new content to later engagement with assumptions and purposes, suggesting an emergent researcher identity. It is personal in the sense that this new perspective on learning has implications for me as tutor in this curricular context. I explore these outcomes, which relate in some ways to the evaluation and research aspects of the study, in more detail in the following sections.

PROGRAMME ORGANIZATION PERSPECTIVES

The layered, dialogic structure of this programme promoted effective learning through combining a broad coverage of the field in input sessions and a focused practical task for the assessment. The structure ensured that students revisited the article and the marked critique, and it also facilitated beneficial encounters with the tutor and peers. The process was effective in supporting dissertation design and completion. Since engaging in this experience with teacher research, we have continued to develop the programme: We have implemented changes relating to the published studies on the list, the introduction of nominated student discussants in the oral presentations, and the use of the institutional Virtual Learning Environment for discussion and dissemination of PowerPoint presentations. The research has illustrated the value of our particular approach and the benefits of our particular programme strategies. However, even though the approach we adopted was clearly effective, we do not suggest that we have developed the definitive research methods course, to be taken off the shelf for delivery by tutors.

GENERAL AND PERSONAL PERSPECTIVES

As described in the literature review section, learning to do research is itself an underresearched field. Few frameworks are elaborated or tested for this form of learning. From this perspective, the view of learning as a process of identity formation has proved fruitful in my attempts to draw together the various strands of the students' experiences of learning to do research. In many cases, the evidence of stages of learning (e.g., see the descriptions of Rudi's experience) suggests that when a sense of shared purpose and procedure develops and is articulated, the student tends to write a good critique and dissertation.

In this chapter, I have described Rudi and others as students. They are also teachers, and the way their learning is situated derives from this particular aspect of their identity. The challenge with a master's in TESOL programme for experienced teachers is to develop a researcher identity which complements the existing teacher identity. After the programme they should be ready to return to the classroom as informed teachers, ready to devise and implement innovative teaching strategies and use teacher research perspectives to understand the benefits and challenges of innovative action. Successful learning thus involves a sense of confidence in both teacher and researcher identities, along with an awareness of how these complement each other as dimensions of their professional role. Finding evidence of such identity development in this study confirms for me the generic rationale for research training in teacher education programmes and the capacity of our programme's teaching strategy to realize this goal.

This demonstrated capacity does not mean that the programme is a definitive product—fixed, accepted, critiqued, no longer characterized by hazy categories, putative interpretations, or speculations. Rather it is a context of ongoing enquiry. I continue to organise and lead the research methods programme, and as a tutor I respond to the same queries time and time again, each time coming up with a new response, framed by what I judge to be the particular context of the student and teacher. Schön (1983) described reflective practice as the way we as professionals learn from repeated engagement with similar problems: the accumulation of problems and solutions are what lead to increasingly effective and expert professional action. The problems and solutions—e-mail queries, written critiques, PowerPoint presentations, videos of oral presentations—are devices stimulating further development of the programme and my understanding of how research methods training is a relevant and essential aspect of teacher development.

Richard Kiely teaches at the University of Bristol in England.

Notes

1. The transcription and analysis of these qualitative data were supported by a Pedagogical Research Grant from the Subject Centre for Languages, Linguistics, and Area Studies of the Learning and Teaching Support Network, supported by the Centre for Information on Language Teaching. I am grateful for the contributions of my colleagues to this phase of the work—Gerald Clibbon, Pauline Rea-Dickins, Helen Woodfield, and Catherine Walter. See Kiely, Clibbon, Rea-Dickins, Walter, and Woodfield (2004) for a detailed account of this phase of the study.

2. Pseudonyms are used for student names throughout this chapter.

CHAPTER 7

Learning to Speak, Speaking to Learn: Research Perspectives on Learner Autonomy Through Collaborative Work in ELT (*Spain*)

Carmen Pérez-Llantada

Issue

As a teacher of English to engineering undergraduates in Spain, one of my main concerns has always been finding ways of encouraging learners to contribute orally in class. However, the traditional transmissive methodology which I adopted in my classes did not seem to encourage learners to talk and participate actively. As a result, at the end of each year most learners were unable to speak English fluently. I then started to pay closer attention to their language learning routines. These were based largely on memorization, drilling, and the repetition of grammatical patterns, leading to the isolated rather than integrated acquisition of language skills. Another noticeable issue was the difficulty learners had in applying what they learned to novel situations, and in identifying language variability across different communicative purposes and contexts of use.

Some teaching trials using a communicative approach (Nunan, 1989; Savignon, 1991) proved to be successful in addressing some of these issues, but even so they laid bare learners' lack of motivation. On a personal level, learners showed no engagement in their learning processes and no interest in finding an efficient way of improving their own language skills. Instead of making day-to-day progress in their communicative competences, they were simply worried about passing exams. Lack of participation in the classroom obviously resulted in a monotonous classroom environment, poor communicative performance, and unsatisfactory academic results. Faced with these observations, I decided to start conducting classroom-based research on two fields of enquiry that are receiving increased attention in the research arena: constructivist theory and learner autonomy. This theoretical background helped to shed light on my initial research question: What pedagogical procedures are suitable in the English language teaching (ELT) classroom to promote learner autonomy and improved language proficiency?

Background Literature

Under the motto "learning through doing," constructivist theory contends that successful knowledge acquisition takes place only when learners are able to retrieve conceptual information and transfer it to practical situations (Duffy & Jonassen, 1992; Jonassen, Ambruso, & Olesen, 1992; Spiro, Feltovich, Jackobson, & Coulson, 1992). As opposed to transmissive procedures in which the teacher is the dominant figure and there is little participation in the classroom, constructivist theorists (Johnson & Johnson, 1991; Kagan, 1992; Slavin, 1985) propose the use of collaborative methodologies as a suitable way of promoting active classroom participation, higher performance, and more autonomous and reflexive knowledge acquisition.

In the past 30 years, learner autonomy has also been a central research and pedagogical concern. The literature on autonomous learning defines it as the type of learning activity in which learners act independently of the teacher and become responsible for their learning progress by developing an awareness of their degree of motivation, learning strategies, and group-building abilities (Scharle & Szabó, 2000). Wolf (1996) remarked that "shared responsibility in the classroom" (p. 51) involves a radical change of attitudes towards classroom management and teacher and learner roles. Other authors such as Ellis and Sinclair (1989) and Oxford (1990) have also examined ways to introduce strategies for individual learning to learners of English. These studies all emphasise the positive effects of learner autonomy in promoting more dynamic and active attitudes in the classroom.

Keeping these theoretical perspectives in mind, two general questions were raised at the initial stage of my research: (1) Do collaborative tasks promote autonomous learning? (2) If so, does improved learner autonomy correlate with more successful language learning and higher proficiency in speaking skills?

Procedures

COURSE DESCRIPTION

The experimental research experience I describe here was carried out in an English for Specific Purposes class of 20 learners who were 20 to 21 years old. This course covered 30 hours during an academic year and was taught in the third year of an undergraduate degree program in electronic engineering at the School of Industrial Engineering at the University of Zaragoza, in Spain. The course aimed to develop speaking skills in English for specialised purposes at an advanced level and, complying with the rationale of the forthcoming European Convergence in Higher Education, sought to train learners in analytical, synthetic, and critical thinking skills as part of the learners' training in academic and professional competence.

PRELIMINARY STEPS

The implementation of a collaborative methodology on this course involved careful planning of learning objectives which covered language, cognitive, and social abilities. Accordingly, the course was developed taking into consideration the learners' particular needs, interests, aptitudes, attitudes, and abilities in relation to the acquisition of integrated competence in academic and professional settings.

The planning stage also involved the development of suitable project-based pedagogical materials. These materials were targeted at improving language proficiency through practice in information transfer, analysis, synthesis, and critical thinking skills. To prompt participation in the oral activities, classroom work was developed around a set of miniprojects. These projects tackled several professional and academic situations and introduced learners to specific aspects of the academic and professional world so that language learning was as close as possible to real-life situations. From a theoretical standpoint, the projects took as a starting point the cognitive principle that knowledge requires the manipulation and interrelatedness of information. As shown in Table 1, the contents of the miniprojects were selected considering the specialised profile of the university degree of the learners; in other words, they were tailor-made to the learners' specific linguistic priorities.

For the purposes of illustration, Table 2 provides a brief sketch of the instructions for one of the projects.

As regards methodological implementation, each miniproject comprised three task-based stages—individual, group, and intergroup tasks—and was intended for a 3-hour session (each stage took approximately 1 hour). The first stage involved individual exposure to conceptual models as well as the analysis and synthesis of information. The second stage sought to elicit speaking skills

Table 1. Topics of the Miniprojects

Project	Type and Scope of the Project
Project 1	A problem-solving activity to be assessed in a business meeting at the Harley-Davidson company headquarters
Project 2	The decision taking on the construction of an oil duct in the Black Sea
Project 3	The process of applying for a university grant and participating in a European university exchange program
Project 4	The development of a laboratory experiment within a technical enterprise devoted to the manufacture of hybrid cars
Project 5	The presentation of a paper/roundtable in an international symposium on new technologies
Project 6	The presentation of a scientific poster in a specialised conference in the area of electronic engineering
Project 7	The creation of individual enterprises and the assessment of a possible merger of the enterprises
Project 8	The preparation of an oral presentation of a research project on alternative energies
Project 9	The assessment of a case study on the feasibility of three electric power stations to cover the demand of 500,000 inhabitants
Project 10	The assessment of an initial technical report on the proposal of the construction of Gibraltar bridge

through meaning reconstruction, information sharing, and information transfer tasks, and was designed to be carried out in groups of four learners. In the third stage, classroom interaction across the different groups focused on developing critical reasoning abilities (Cederblom & Paulsen, 2001), thus involving higher level knowledge manipulation. All the tasks were based on problem-solving work, case studies, role plays, or simulation activities, and their main goal was to further oral and integrated skills through activities involving induction, deduction, construction of support, criticism, and assessment of information.

DATA COLLECTION

Research conducted during the 2004–2005 academic year was targeted at quantifying and qualifying the extent to which collaborative work helps learners develop more autonomous learning styles, thus making them more proficient when communicating in English. At the beginning of the course, learners took a pretest that measured their written and spoken skills on a scale from 1 to 10 (see

Table 2. Instructions for Project 8

Project 8. Alternative Energies
Individual task (computer-based assignment): Watch the video "Electricity for the Future" (Scientific Eye, video series from the UK's public service station, Channel 4) which describes different alternative energies, and write down a summary of the key ideas explained in the video. Your next task is to carry out a general search on alternative energies. Access http://www.energyquest.ca.gov/story/index.html, find out information about one specific type of alternative energy, and write a short synthesis about it. Once you have finished, send your documents by e-mail to the instructor.
Group task (information exchange activity in small groups): In turns, explain to the members of your group what you have learnt about the alternative energy you selected for the individual task. When you finish, write a joint report providing a brief description of the four types of alternative energies you have been discussing together.
Intergroup task (role play, the five groups together; instructions are given as homework so that the students can prepare their expositions in advance): You are attending an international meeting on renewable energies in Tokyo, Japan. With your group, you have to give an oral presentation arguing in favour of one specific type of alternative energy at the conference. Give your talk and be ready for the audience's questions and counterarguments.

Appendix). This scale covers grammatical, discourse, sociolinguistic, and strategic competence (Canale & Swain, 1980). To obtain comparative results, learners took a similar test at the end of the course; the rating criteria were the same for the posttest and pretest.

Another source of data was a learner corpus. Using a corpus, the teacher can obtain quantitative evidence about specific aspects of language performance (Biber & Conrad, 2001; Granger, 1998; Granger, Hung, & Petch-Tyson, 2002; Hunston, 2002). As for the specifics of my research, I now explain the typology, design, and production of the learner corpus compiled.

First, I collected a written subcorpus to assess individual second language performance in the first phase of the miniprojects. Learners submitted their essays by e-mail, and a total of 10 written documents per learner—one per project—formed the portfolio or dossier of personal documents. The assessment scale included in the Appendix also applied to these individual portfolios across the four language competences.

I then compiled a second written subcorpus to evaluate the effectiveness of group work in the second stage of the miniprojects. In this phase, learners had to comment on individual proposals, reach a consensus, and generate a joint document taking into account the opinions of all the members of the group. This activity entailed integrated skills practice based on information transfer, analysis, synthesis, and interpretation. Five group assignments per project made a total of

50 written records, and were also rated using the previously mentioned assessment scale.

Finally, I created a third subcorpus with videotapes of the students' oral presentations that they had to prepare in the last stage of the miniprojects. As noted earlier, the intergroup activities used in the third phase of the projects required critical reasoning skills through tasks such as induction, deduction, analysis, and assessment of individual and group perspectives. Every member of the group in turn had to argue in favour of the written proposal generated by their group in stage two of the projects. A total of 10 hours of presentation work was recorded to rate individual and group performance across the four language competences. The rating process used the same scale employed for the two written subcorpora.

Apart from these measurable parameters, I used other procedures to gather additional information on the research experience: my observations, informal conversations with the learners throughout the academic year, and a questionnaire handed out at the end of the course. The questionnaire was designed to assess learners' opinions about the appropriateness of this new methodology and their new role as autonomous learners. These sources provided further insight into learners' awareness of their language learning routines and strategies, and their degree of autonomy, motivation, and responsibility in relation to learning English.

Results

LEARNERS' PERFORMANCE

Figure 1 compares the means of the learners' academic results across written and spoken skills from the pretest and the posttest. As one might expect, students scored higher grades at the end of the year. However, listening and speaking abilities—in which learners did poorly (less than 4.0) in the initial test—displayed considerably better results (a difference of 4.8 and 5.4 points, respectively) in the final test. These data suggest that, by promoting knowledge manipulation, participation, and more responsible attitudes towards day-to-day progress, collaborative work supports improved language proficiency when learning to speak a language.

The rating of the three subcorpora (individual portfolios, group reports, and intergroup presentations) also provided important information about learners' gradual improvement in the acquisition of the four language competences. As illustrated in Extracts 1 and 2—examples from coursework—learners showed linguistic competence at the end of the course through a confident handling of syntactic structures and a wide range of general and technical vocabulary. They made fewer grammatical errors and became linguistically fluent in producing stretches of language. Learners' discourse competence in written and spoken

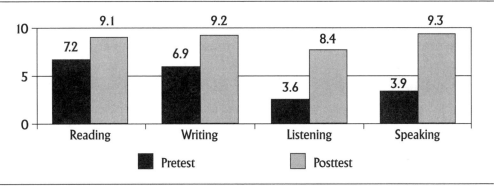

Figure 1. Pretest and posttest scores on four language skills.

production also revealed an appropriate organisation of paragraphs and texts (through techniques such as definitions, descriptions, comparisons and contrasts, exemplification, and cause/effect relationships) and a logically sequenced linkage of ideas for cohesion and coherence purposes:

Extract 1 (Written Production)
Computers consist of several thousands of integrated circuits that are used to control industrial operations and supervise the management systems of businesses and enterprises. In industry, for instance, integrated circuits serve as the brains of industrial robots like mechanical arms, and are able to carry out complex operations, from a painting process to the assembly of the different components of modern cars, with high precision.

Extract 2 (Spoken Production)
The determination of the alteration factor caused by reflection is a complex issue that falls within the scope of spectrophotometry, as this is the field that studies the reflections across chromatic graphs. Now, I am going to carry out several procedures to determine the alteration factor on a particular reflecting surface. To do so, I will first begin with a 7-minute exposure and then I will follow with a series of five consecutive tests in equal intervals of 1 or 2 minutes.

Together with grammatical and discourse proficiency, learners showed progress in sociolinguistic aspects of the language. Against an initial poor competence in these skills, learners developed an awareness of communication elements in the different role-plays and simulations they enacted (different participants, types of events, settings, social identities, and power relations). Learners also showed sensitivity to register mode; that is, they learnt to choose adequate syntax and vocabulary (a more formal and elaborate style for writing, and a more informal, simplified, and personal style for speaking, as shown in Extracts 1 and 2).

With reference to strategic communication, the videotaped subcorpus allowed the identification of resources that learners gradually acquired for effective communication. For instance, they learnt to produce rules of interaction similar to those observed in linguistic models and to use correct pronunciation and prosodic elements in speech, such as intonation, stress and chunking, emphasis, pauses, and body language. They also used strategies such as repetition of ideas, clarification, paraphrasing, and reformulation to facilitate the audience's comprehension. Extract 3 illustrates these points.

Extract 3 (Spoken Production)
Some of these rays, those infrared rays, [repetition and clarification] can escape to the outer space, but [stressed and followed by a pause] some of them are absorbed by the greenhouse gases. Greenhouse gases [repetition] aren't able to absorb solar rays, but they do [stressed] absorb infrared rays and after that they heat the things towards them. In other words, [reformulation] some of the infrared rays are absorbed by those "teeny weeny" [emphasis added] molecules and those molecules heat everything around them.

In all, the steady upward trend shown in the scores learners achieved on their project assignments throughout the academic year suggests that these projects promoted language learning effectively. Quantitatively speaking, Figure 2 displays the comparative means across the four language competences scored in the individual, group, and intergroup assignments of Project 1 (at the beginning of the course), Project 5 (midterm), and Project 10 (at the end of the course). Against poor-to-average sociolinguistic and strategic competences and an average discourse mastery shown in the rating of Project 1 at the beginning of the course, the means obtained in Project 10 at the end of the course indicate much more satisfactory results (8.1 to 9.1 out of 10 points).

To sum up, this research shows that, by favouring a more flexible learning environment that allowed active participation and more responsibility in the learning process, collaborative work promoted more effective language learning.

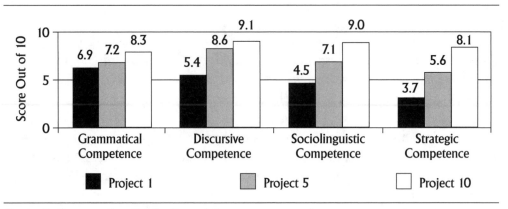

Figure 2. Comparative distribution of the means across language competences.

TEACHER'S OBSERVATIONS AND LEARNERS' VIEWS

Apart from the performance results discussed previously, data from my own observations, from conversations with learners, and from a questionnaire they completed provided further insight into the processes promoted by the collaborative project-based methodology used on the course.

Teacher's Observations

From my observations, I identified a number of ways in which learners benefited from the approach we adopted. First, on a conceptual level the construction of knowledge took account of "higher degrees of interconnectedness" (Spiro et al., 1992, p. 62). I felt that as the teacher I successfully contextualised all the conceptual elements taught in the course. The presentation of concepts in different contexts of use furthered understanding of language structures through processes of reasoning and inference. Through comprehension, learners identified those structures that are more prominent in each type of communicative event or situation. Through interpretation, they discovered why these structures are used and what they are used for in a particular communicative situation. Only by deducing and reasoning about the real use of the language did they put into practice language concepts in "socially acceptable terms" (Bourdieu, 2001, p. 508). Instead of learning linguistic concepts in an isolated and repetitive way, course participants learnt to analyse, interpret, and, most important, retrieve and use those concepts in different specific situations.

Additionally, on a psychocognitive level, classroom management validated Skehan's (1998) proposal of a "rich instruction approach" (p. 44). With collaborative methodology, learners first received frequent and relevant linguistic input, so they focused on conceptual aspects which were significant for them to communicate effectively in the foreign language. Once learners recognised these conceptual elements as relevant, cooperative work elicited the analysis and transfer of this new conceptual knowledge to novel situations. These cognitive procedures ensured a more effective acquisition of language competences.

Task-based collaborative work built up other cognitive strategies such as information search and synthesis. Learners were trained in finding information quickly and confidently, in grasping the general meaning, and in deciding what information is relevant to carrying out the tasks. These strategies in turn favoured more realistic integrated language skills practice. Similarly, the critical thinking activities of the miniprojects generated observation and interpretation, reasoning and inference, and valuing and judging. The development of critical reasoning through group cooperation contributed to more active use of English for problem solving and reflective practice.

On a personal level, learners' initial lack of motivation gave way to a deeper commitment to learning English. Collaborative work paved the way for active learner participation, for example, when distributing roles and tasks, taking decisions and sharing opinions, and, more broadly, communicating with others. This new attitude engaged learners in a more thorough and efficient use of integrated language skills through simulated practices that demanded identifying problems, leading projects, assessing risks, and providing efficient solutions.

Teacher-learner relationships were also positively affected by the implementation of a constructivist and collaborative methodology. Students learnt to seek the help of the teacher in and outside the classroom. In doing so, they received adequate feedback and solved problems. Learning to be critical also helped them confront problems in their learning processes, reflect deeply on their learning attitudes, and develop insights into their own language learning strategies. Such attributes are important in the development of learner autonomy.

There were also benefits on a social level, because group work addressed what Arnold (1999) described as the cognitive and affective sides of learning. Participants learnt to share information, listen and be attentive to others, and reach a consensus. Within the group they shared targets and resources, became responsible for their roles, and learned that they could not succeed unless the whole group succeeded. Consistent with recent studies in ELT research (Morita, 2004; Nakahama, Tyler, & van Lier, 2001; Nakatani, 2002), group work gave learners opportunities to shape their own learning styles, negotiate their positioning, and construct their identities in class. Also, the heterogeneity of the group supported the development of more tolerant and critical stances towards each member's learning routines. In short, collaborative methods led to observable improvements in learners' social behaviour.

Learners' Perceptions

Informal conversations with learners during the academic year indicated how, in a collaborative methodology, the teacher's responsibility is reduced in favour of learner autonomy. The following two extracts from learners' informal talk are indicative of the way collaborative work promotes autonomous, more responsible, and self-reflexive learning behaviours. In the first excerpt the learner (S1)—whose precourse test scores were very low—commented that he felt very comfortable with the methodological approach and showed interest in overcoming his difficulties in the language. Less than two months into the course, he showed a responsible attitude towards learning, requesting feedback from his teacher to check his progress.

> S1: I've always been very bad at English, but this year I like the subject much more, the way you teach it, and I'm making a great effort. I would like to talk to you so that you can tell me what you think about my knowledge of the subject and my performance in class.

A few weeks later, another learner (S2) seemed to be unhappy with the marks he had received and decided to talk with me (T) during the class break. In my role of advisor, I tried to guide the learner to make him aware of his undesirable learning behaviours and his attitude towards learning the language. Significantly, the learner pointed out his own weaknesses (lack of interest, not much time spent doing the classroom tasks, no use of either backup materials or teacher's counselling). At the end of the conversation, the learner overtly decided to change his attitude, thus developing a more responsible stance:

S2: I've always had good marks in this subject, I know a lot of English, but now my marks are all very low, and I don't understand why.

T: How's that? What do you think?

S2: Well, I thought my written essays and my oral presentations were okay, but . . . well, to tell you the truth, I do not spend much time, I do things quite fast and I don't revise them.

T: Do you use grammars and dictionaries to help? Do you use a spell checker to correct the spelling and grammar mistakes of your compositions? You can use them, they're very useful. You can also come to office hours to revise, check, and find more help whenever you want.

S2: No [answering the teacher's questions]. Last day, in the presentation of alternative energies I was given the part which was more difficult to explain, and I know that I did not explain it very well, it doesn't come out, same as the compositions, they don't come out because I did not prepare them, I did not have time to prepare them in advance.

T: Don't worry, it's good that you are aware of these things, we still have time to solve the problem. What can you do?

S2: Can I rewrite and repeat all the tasks we've done so far, this time doing them okay? Will you check them again? And I do not want you to modify my marks if I do them better now.

These more mature attitudes were difficult to observe among the learners when collaborative methods had not previously been used in the classroom. Yet such mature attitudes became frequent in the early stages of this course and were good indicators of greater learner autonomy, responsibility, and motivation.

The questionnaire on learner autonomy and cooperative work at the end of the year also provided interesting data on learners' feelings about their learning experiences. When asked about the extent to which they had improved their language skills, all the learners said they were very satisfied or satisfied with their results. The learners also reported responsible learning behaviours—use of additional study hours, additional materials, and office hours; and sustained effort to learn—as well as a positive response towards collaborative classroom procedures. Learners stated that although cooperative work required greater effort in the performance of the assignments, it nonetheless allowed them more autonomy and creativity—attitudes which they defined as very profitable for them. In addition, they said they had learnt cognitive abilities such as managing tasks, analysing language acquisition problems, and identifying ways of responding to these problems.

Learners also pointed out the acquisition of social abilities in problem-solving and decision-making tasks, as well as the development of trust and leadership within the group. Peer interaction was a positively evaluated learning resource; learners said they had learnt to communicate, to respect others' opinions, to make concessions, to be more tolerant, and to develop abilities of self-confidence and efficacy in the group.

At the end of the course, the learners were also asked to evaluate the extent to which they felt they had developed more autonomous and reflexive language learning strategies. On a scale from 1 to 10, they were asked to evaluate the following:

- Level of linguistic proficiency

- Awareness of learning routines and use of cognitive strategies

- Degree of development of autonomous learning styles

- Development of social competence

The results were consistently high across the 20 learners, with self-assessments ranging from 7 to 10 on all four issues. These data suggest not only that a collaborative methodology was received very positively by learners but also that it helped learners to articulate a practical vision of their behaviour as autonomous learners and to become efficient in taking initiative and generating constructive social stances.

Overall, taking into account data from the assessment of learners' work, my observations, the questionnaire data, and informal conversations and feedback from learners, I conclude that the collaborative and constructivist project-based approach created suitable conditions for language learning (particularly orally) and for the development of learner autonomy and enhanced motivation.

Reflection

Doing this study has allowed me to confirm my belief in the benefits for teaching and learning of doing classroom research. Through this project I was able to engage with a problem that I had been aware of for many years and to experiment with practical pedagogical strategies for addressing it. The results are encouraging because they indicate that the methodological approach I adopted did in fact have a positive effect on many aspects of language learning, including learners' performance in using the language. Learners' attitudes towards learning English and their motivation to learn were much more positive with this group of learners than with any other group I had previously taught using more conventional language learning methodologies.

Although the picture one may get from this chapter is very positive, I should point out that conducting this type of research involves an initial effort to prepare suitable materials and ongoing commitment (over the course of a year in this case) to collect and carefully analyse data. Classroom research for teachers, then, though rewarding, is also challenging. This is, however, a challenge that we teachers need to take on if we are really concerned about finding better ways to teach languages to learners. Only by taking responsibility for our own professional development in this way will we be in a better position to bridge the gap between research and teaching activities or, as Swales (2002) metaphorically calls it, between integrated and fragmented worlds.

Carmen Pérez-Llantada teaches at the University of Zaragoza, Spain.

Appendix: Assessment Scale for Written/Spoken Work

INDICATORS OF GRAMMATICAL COMPETENCE

1. Accurate linguistic expression. Few syntactic errors, and confident handling of appropriate structures (agreement, tense, number, word order, articles, pronouns, prepositions, etc.).

2. Elaborate language and great variety of syntactic patterning. Grammatical constructions are adequate for the communicative purposes of the text/speech. Wide range of vocabulary, both general and specialised. Accurate word choice and usage.

3. Fluent expression. Capacity to produce stretches of language easily and, in speech, to cope with real-time communication.

4. Full command of spelling, punctuation, capitalisation, layout.

INDICATORS OF DISCOURSE COMPETENCE

5. The text/speech moves from general to particular or uses a problem-solving pattern. Appropriate organisation of paragraphs, and logically sequenced (coherence). Adequate treatment of the subject; the treatment of various subtopics is balanced. Variety of ideas or argument.

6. Ideas clearly stated and supported. Use of rhetorical techniques (descriptions, definitions, classifications, comparison and contrasts, reason/result argumentation, etc.). Correct use of discourse markers indicating the flow of information. Connectives appropriately used (cohesion).

7. Visual elements accompanying the text/speech are used correctly and serve to convey rhetorical purposes.

INDICATORS OF SOCIOLINGUISTIC COMPETENCE

8. Sensitivity to register (either written or spoken) and adoption of the correct style. Appropriate selection of syntax and vocabulary (lexicogrammar) within the scope of the register.

9. Writer/speaker's awareness of communication elements (participants, type of event, setting, enactment of social identity, power relations, etc.).

10. Correct use of interpersonal language: when required, either the writer/speaker's opinion is conveyed overtly or the writer/speaker contrives to remain anonymous.

INDICATORS OF STRATEGIC COMPETENCE

11. Ability to produce similar rules of interaction to those observed in linguistic models. In written/spoken work, use of techniques for effective communication (repetition of ideas, clarification, reformulation, paraphrases, etc.).

12. In speech, no slips of grammar, halts and hesitation, loss of memory, etc. Ability to cope with communication difficulties such as distractions or background noise.

13. Correct use of pronunciation. Other prosodic aspects such as pace of the delivery, intonation, stress, emphasis, chunking, repetition, and pauses are used correctly. Use of body language to facilitate speech processing.

CHAPTER 8

Meeting CEF Standards: Research Action in Local Action Research (*Italy*)

Anna Franca Plastina

When a practitioner becomes a researcher into his own practice, he engages in a continuing process of self-education. When she functions as a researcher-in-practice, the practice itself is a source of renewal. (Schön, 1983, p. 299)

Issue

This investigation into the teacher educator's role in institutional projects began with my involvement in the Italian national teacher research project designated Ricerca delle Competenze (RIC-CO), that is, research on competencies. The project was launched with the purpose of fostering the development of a national foreign language curriculum, based on the assumption that the *Common European Framework of Reference for Languages* (Council of Europe, 2001), or CEF, performance descriptors are suitable objectives to set for the language learning paths of the Italian educational system. Over the course of 2 years, the project engaged language teacher educators, in-service foreign language teachers, and students in investigating the CEF standards in Italian classrooms through action research (AR). Even though the national quantitative study aimed to measure Italian students' language proficiency levels, a local AR tryout was carried out by provincial groups with the support of language teacher educators. The subsequent qualitative research aimed at investigating whether individual teaching processes are calibrated to attain CEF standards, enabling groups of in-service teachers to explore their pedagogical practice.

Working as a teacher educator with a local group of teachers in Calabria, in southern Italy, was for me a valuable opportunity to receive new professional stimuli from the two research paths—national and local—of the RIC-CO project. From the outset, however, it seemed to me that this macroinitiative placed major emphasis on the collection, tabulation, and analysis of quantitative testing data by the local groups in order to create a ministerial database about Italian foreign language pedagogy in relation to European standards. Minor attention was given to local qualitative research, which was carried out with the support of prescribed AR tools, designed by a national team of academic experts involved in the project.

In this context, I perceived that the teacher educator was expected to supervise the accomplishment of research study according to prescribed procedures and deadlines rather than to advise the AR group on teacher researcher development. This fact led me to reflect on the interrelation between the prescribed AR tools and the research group, and to engage in a systematic self-inquiry process once I had received the set of AR tools developed centrally through the larger project. Self-inquiry appeared all the more necessary when I became aware that the national instructions focused only on what to implement in the local AR tryout rather than on how to do so. How I would suitably introduce the AR tools to facilitate teachers' understanding of their functional use became a major issue when I realised that the 11 English as a foreign language (EFL) in-service teachers in the group were all traditional teachers with no preservice training, no practical experience of AR, and little theoretical CEF knowledge. Coming from a cross-grade teaching background (primary, lower, and upper secondary) and different provincial workplaces, all participants had applied to the RIC-CO project to further their professional development. The challenge was, therefore, to engage in a self-inquiry process which would bring to the surface an understanding of my role in supporting the potential teacher researchers in taking responsibility for their local actions with a European mindset in the 40 hours allotted to the project. In the literature, the role of the teacher educator in supporting teacher researcher development has been frequently discussed.

Background Literature

A contemporary position in teacher education is that "the role of the teacher educator is no longer simply that of a trainer" (Richards, 1990, p. 15) who, as a supervisor and expert, transmits knowledge and skills to teachers considered as passive recipients of information. More than equipping teachers with knowledge and models of best practice, teacher educators should employ enabling procedures (Prabhu, 1987) to support teachers in developing a self-inquiry attitude towards their often routinised classroom practices. This is possible only if teacher educators adopt a research ownership approach, whereby they investigate their community of practice, seeking understanding into its three dimensions: (1) what it is about, (2) how it functions, and (3) what capability it has produced (Wenger, 1998).

It follows that teacher educators need to become insiders of the event, capturing the richness of teacher researcher beliefs and practices and the complexity of classroom dynamics. Even when engaged in institutional projects, teacher educators should strongly encourage teachers to take a research stance, whereby they are "engaged in a process of refining, and becoming more autonomous in, professional judgement" (Hopkins, 1985, p. 3). This implies that teacher educators trigger development by raising teacher awareness rather than through direct intervention (Freeman, 1989) and hand over the responsibility for the exploration of the actual pedagogical processes employed to the teachers. Thus as facilitators, collaborators, and coparticipants of such events, teacher educators promote learning experiences which move beyond training (Richards & Nunan, 1990). Among these experiences, action research can be considered a valuable opportunity to enhance teacher education. As Kemmis and McTaggart (1992) noted, AR is

> not the usual thinking teachers do when they think about their teaching because it is more systematic and collaborative; it is not simply problem-solving because it also involves problem-posing; it is not research done on other people because it is done by oneself on one's own work. (p. 10)

In supporting teachers' exploration, development, and reflection on their teaching (Head & Taylor, 1997), data gathering and analysis become central to action research, whereby teachers are assisted in uncovering their own "implicit assumptions about teaching, learning, and schooling" (Cochran-Smith & Lytle, 1990, p. 4). AR tools, thus, play an important role in determining (a) what data to collect for specific self-inquiry, (b) how the processes for data collection are organised and conducted, and (c) which specific actions are consistently taken to enhance data analysis and self-reflection. By exploiting the full value of the research tools at their disposal through a research ownership approach, teacher educators gain a deep understanding of their beliefs and practices, which ultimately benefit teacher researchers.

Procedures

The aim of the present self-inquiry was to study whether an exploration of the functional meaning and use of prescribed AR tools would affect the teacher educator's local action of supporting teacher researchers. My inquiry into this issue was structured around three distinct phases of my work with these teachers: (1) preliminary, (2) in-class action, (3) recall. In the week preceding my first meeting with the AR group (preliminary phase), my inquiry centred around the AR tools and quantitative testing materials I had been given. This phase addressed the following research question: How could the AR tools be systematised and selected to support teachers in understanding their functional meaning and use in order to appropriately explore research objectives? The second phase covered the 6-week period of in-class teacher education. Self-inquiry during this phase was based on the following research question: What did I learn from introducing specific actions to induce teacher reflection through the use of specific AR tools? In the recall phase (1 week) when all project commitments were accomplished, self-inquiry focused on recalling meaningful features which had affected my overall feelings about the AR tools. During the recall phase, I considered the following research question: How did such inquiry improve my professional competence?

I collected introspective data over the 8 weeks covering the three research phases through intrapersonal journal writing. Intrapersonal journals, that is, a series of first-person accounts of the undergoing event, have been discussed as a valid means of reflective teacher development (Gebhard, 1999). Journal entries included annotations on plans, thoughts, feelings, and observations which solicited internal decisions as understood from my viewpoint. I made the entries using a stream-of-consciousness writing style, which allowed me to jot down reflective notes freely and quickly. Moreover, I used this process because it "does not require that we have highly sophisticated empirical skills" (Gebhard & Oprandy, 1999, p. 74). As both the author and recipient of my journal entries, I reviewed significant introspective data related to the research questions at the end of each self-inquiry phase (Bailey, 1990).

I collected qualitative information from group discussions with the teachers during the in-class action phase. In guiding the teachers in spontaneous discussions, I encouraged them to freely express their perceptions, attitudes, and beliefs related to their pedagogical practice. Relevant information, which provided insights into not just what the teachers thought but why they thought it, was recorded as journal entries in this phase.

I analysed the data under the following headings, which corresponded to the stages I went through in making sense of the AR tools I received and in supporting teachers' understanding and use of these tools:

- Phase 1—classifying and selecting the AR tools

- Phase 2—in-class actions (by the teacher educator or teacher researcher) related to the AR tools

- Phase 3—identification of a professional development pattern underlying the implementation of the AR tools

Results

PHASE 1: CLASSIFYING AND SELECTING THE AR TOOLS

I received a set of AR tools developed centrally as part of the larger project I referred to earlier, and I was encouraged to support teachers in using these in their own classrooms. The tools were the following:

- A teacher researcher biography data sheet

- A school biography data sheet

- A perception questionnaire

- Open-ended questionnaires for each language competency area (oral interaction, listening, reading, writing) for the teacher researchers' use

- Open-ended questionnaires for each language competency area for the learners' use (designed in a more user friendly way for the younger learners)

- Closed questionnaires for each language competency area for the teacher researchers' use

- Closed questionnaires for each language competency area for the learners' use

- A classroom observation grid

- Lesson feedback sheets for the learners' use

- Lesson recall sheets for the teacher researchers' use

These tools were not classified in any particular way, and during the first stage of my work I analysed them and considered ways of systematically classifying them. I felt that presenting the tools in an organised way would help the teachers more easily make sense of them.

Classification

After analysing the tools, I grouped them into five categories (as shown in Table 1): (1) institutional data sheets, (2) semisubjective research tools, (3) objective research tools, (4) direct observation tools, (5) indirect observation tools.

The school and teacher researcher biography data sheets are institutional tools which support the collection of bureaucratic information for the national project database. As such, they cannot be directly considered as pure teacher researcher tools. At a local level, however, I believe they can offer a wealth of information. As a source for group discussion, institutional data sheets can help me develop an understanding of how to adjust to the research group's needs. The semisubjective tools, designed by the academic experts as four open-ended questionnaires (*questionari aperti*), elicit reflective opinions on the four language skills as seen by the teachers and learners.

By analysing the purpose of these tools, I realised how important it is for teachers to collect data not only on language competency but also on the ongoing AR experience. I then decided I would encourage the group to use a purely subjective research tool such as a personal log to enhance their understandings of the AR processes they were being encouraged to adopt.

Two objective research tools—a perception questionnaire and teacher/learner language competency closed questionnaires (*questionari chiusi*)—supported the collection of more observable data. The perception questionnaire targeted teachers' perceptions of their professional knowledge and principles as well as their teaching practices and styles. This tool could help me trigger teacher reflection on *received* knowledge (theoretical principles) and *experiential* knowledge (practical teaching experience). In particular, it could aid me in guiding the teachers to delve deeper into their unconscious routinised actions and gain awareness of

Table 1. Functional Classification of the AR Tools

Institutional Data Sheets	Semisubjective	Objective	Direct Observation	Indirect Observation
Teacher researcher biography data sheet	Teacher/learner language competency open-ended questionnaires	Perception questionnaire	Classroom observation grid	Lesson recall sheet for teachers
School biography data sheet		Teacher/learner language competency closed questionnaires		Lesson feedback sheet for learners

their rooted beliefs. By interpreting their professional self-perceptions, the teachers would, I believed, eventually move away from their stereotyped role models.

The classroom observation grid was a direct observation tool, structured as a Communicative Orientation of Language Teaching (COLT) grid (Allen, Fröhlich, & Spada, 1984). It was, in fact, a time-based checklist, coded with a category system in macrocategories (time, activity, language, classroom dynamics, language content, learning modality, tools, and materials) and relative subcategories which are ticked off as snapshot instances of action. The structure of the COLT grid appeared to me as an objective and closed research tool because no subjective exploratory annotations could be made. Although the use of the COLT grid was not compulsory, I thought that the opportunity to introduce such a tool would prove valuable for various reasons. First, because the teachers had no preservice training background, they would engage in a first-time experience of classroom observation which would certainly offer them professional enrichment. Second, they could cross-check COLT data with indirect observation results (teacher's lesson recall sheets, learners' lesson feedback sheets) for a more coherent action research. Lastly, I could lead them to grasp the full meaning of the macro- and subcategories, both as COLT parameters and as theoretical principles.

Selection

Once I had classified the AR tools, I needed to decide which ones to introduce to the teachers and which aspects of classroom learning to encourage teachers to examine. The education ministry stipulated that participating teachers had to implement all the tools except the COLT grid, which was optional, and that the full range of language competencies had to be investigated. However, I found that it was important for me to reflect on these requirements in light of my knowledge of the local contexts in which the teachers I was working with would be using the AR tools. For example, I was aware that the teachers would have limited time and no prior experience of AR. Thus, I believed that it would be more effective to require teachers to conduct a small-scale intervention on only one problematic competency area. I felt that this would equip the AR novices with a methodological background to self-inquiry skills and provide them with a model of the research experience.

I also considered the selection of the COLT grid in terms of teachers' decision making. I hypothesised that the teachers would manifest self-consciousness and anxiety about being observed for the first time after a long teaching experience. Nevertheless, I was convinced that the subsequent professional growth was worth the challenge. I realised that to overcome this problem, I could lead them beforehand to (a) act as observers of a video-recorded lesson during an in-class COLT simulation, (b) understand the importance of assuming an objective rather than a biased attitude towards observing, and (c) decide autonomously to be observed in their classrooms and to personally choose their observers.

Thus, Phase 1 of the research process involved me, as a teacher educator, in reflecting on the objectives and materials which had been defined centrally and which I was expected to follow. During this phase, by examining the nature of the AR tools I received and reflecting on the teachers I would be working with, I made decisions about (a) which AR tools would be presented, (b) how they would be presented, and (c) how teachers could most profitably be encouraged to work with these materials in exploring the CEF in their own classrooms.

PHASE 2: IN-CLASS ACTION OUTCOMES

In this phase, in-class teacher education took place over 6 weeks and was arranged in five in-class sessions (4 hours per session) to support the teachers in developing self-inquiry skills to implement AR and administer quantitative testing materials in the 20-hour self-study time allotted.

During the first session and following the completion of the institutional data sheets, I took the lead in encouraging group members to freely share their bureaucratic information in a brief group discussion. I moderated the discussion with the aim of inducing participants to practise overtly expressing their feelings, establish empathy so as to delve more deeply into their true professional identities, and create a friendly research climate. My journal entries in this early phase of our work recorded information about participants' professional qualifications, background knowledge, and work environment. Data from the discussion recorded individual fears, needs, and expectations about the AR project. Not only had my self-inquiry provided me with useful information to set up a collaborative community of inquiry and adjust to its needs, but it mostly helped me gain understanding of the importance of attending to individual strengths and qualities rather than emphasising deficiencies. I learned to reserve judgment as a way to sustain the group.

During the second in-class session, when the group members were discussing their feelings about doing AR and sharing issues deriving from self-study readings, one teacher researcher introduced a train journey metaphor for the AR process. Like passengers departing for a European destination with their personal luggage, the teacher researchers would meet new people, stop at different stations, and travel through the darkness of tunnels, alternated with daylight. The metaphor provoked thought with its clear image, creating a sense of coherence about what we were doing. The teacher researchers referred to the metaphor in various occasions, especially when it helped them assume a more optimistic attitude to overcome the tunnel phases. The metaphor proved particularly useful when each AR tool was introduced, because we were aware of where we stood along the common journey. As I learned, metaphors contributed by participants helped them establish clear research directions (Woodward, 1991).

During the following sessions, concrete action was sought to understand the European objectives of the project. I invited teachers to verify their competencies, state their language learning priorities, and set future language learning goals by using the Association of Language Testers in Europe (ALTE)[1] can-do checklists. I learned that by implementing such action, I avoided overwhelming teachers with theoretical notions about the bulky CEF framework (Council of Europe, 2001); helped them to become aware of the CEF focus on learners' language needs, self-assessment, and autonomy; and guided them to rethink their classroom practice from a can-do perspective. As a result, the teacher researchers used the outcomes of the can-do checklists to calibrate their language proficiency levels to one of the six CEF levels—basic: A1/A2; independent: B1/B2; proficient: C1/C2.

I further learned that step-by-step guidance as teachers moved from the use of a CEF self-assessment grid to a CEF global scale helped them assimilate the learner-centred approach of the CEF *I can* descriptors. In triggering teacher reflection on the evaluation and descriptors, I facilitated an exploitation of the CEF subskills. Teachers started to speculate on how they could practically use the CEF subskills as self-contained chunks of learning to design their syllabus objectives. The practical action had also developed reassurance that no specific prescriptive methods were considered effective at the CEF level. Overall, I learned that CEF analysis had been useful in stimulating teacher awareness of the importance of extending teaching practice beyond linguistic competence to include pragmatic, sociolinguistic, intercultural, strategic, and existential competence (Heyworth, 2004).

While teachers were keeping personal logs, one teacher researcher encouraged group members to share their recorded thoughts aloud in class. This initiative reinforced collaborative construction of action and improved community rapport. My decision to introduce personal logs had proved helpful in triggering teacher action in sharing doubts and uncertainties. Above all, it had stimulated the teachers to move from intrapersonal inquiry towards interpersonal reflection.

When the teachers carried out self-perceptive inquiry, I felt the need to collaborate as an insider in the process. I took the action of self-disclosure (Egan, 2000), whereby I confided my inner professional ideals, limitations, and struggles, which eventually had a liberating effect on the teachers. I noticed how they gradually released their initial fears and anxieties as a result of my self-disclosure and how this action had contributed to building a safe and supportive atmosphere.

Reflecting on triangulation, that is, the data sets obtained from three viewpoints (teacher researcher, learner, classroom observer) was another important action. I realised that triangulating data not only enhanced validity and minimized bias, but also triggered comparative community reflection and stimulated curiosity about different workplaces.

The action of simulating in-class observations helped me gain insight into two issues. Firstly, the teachers were not completely familiar with the coded category system of the COLT grid. By stressing the conceptual labels of the macro- and microcategories, I led them to develop the habit of using a professional metalanguage rather than vague generic statements which could lead to miscommunication. Secondly, when 10 teachers decided to engage in classroom observation (one was overburdened with daily commitments), I attempted to interpret how they had chosen their observers. In a group discussion held after the in-class simulation, 7 teachers decided to rely on their AR fellows, saying they believed these teachers were now acquainted with proper data recording. They also aimed to extend the benefits of the experience through in-class discussion and reflection on the data collected. I understood that the teacher researchers' inquiry skills were developing, and they desired to be observed by equally competent professionals.

Two teachers took a different approach and self-recorded their classroom events on video. Subsequently, they carried out COLT self-observation, firmly believing that external observers would affect classroom dynamics with their young learners. Then they took the initiative of triangulating their data with those from their perception questionnaires and with the outcomes of an in-class group observation session based on their videos. I learned that the two teacher researchers were taking a leading role in soliciting group action and autonomous self-inquiry. Another teacher researcher decided to involve an EFL colleague from the same workplace because the school location was too distant for fellow researchers. This caused the observee extra preliminary effort in instructing the peer teacher on the use of the COLT grid. This decision, however, led to the action of planning and implementing a similar research programme extended to all teachers of that school. In the long run, the practical constraints had indirectly facilitated the teacher researcher's initiative in using her workplace to cascade her educational experience.

PHASE 3: RECALL FINDINGS

In this phase, the data I recorded in my journal focused on the extent to which my AR decisions and actions in Phases 1 and 2 had improved my professional competence. By analysing the sequential implementation of the AR tools, I attempted to uncover a possible underlying pattern of teacher development which would make me aware of my professional competence. Firstly, I had decided on the use of personal logs as a subjective research tool to record ongoing AR reflective processes. Subsequently, I had guided the teachers to use the perception questionnaire to gain conscious professional identity and to explicitly express their beliefs. A focus on open-ended and closed questionnaires was the next step to determine teachers' viewpoints on language competencies, and teachers mirrored that step by using questionnaires to determine learners' perspectives on the issue. Through the use of the COLT observation grid, the teacher researchers then placed attention on classroom behaviour. The overall instructional environment was subsequently recorded through teacher's recall sheets and learners' feedback sheets. This sequential use of the AR tools made me realise that there are different levels of self-inquiry and that I had guided the research group to move from the inner to the outer levels. Table 2 illustrates the professional development pattern which I identified and which I had tried to promote during my work with the teachers.

Overall, my reflections on the processes I followed in supporting teachers in their AR projects enhanced my professional understanding of three main points:

1. It is important to guide teacher researchers in self-inquiry practice which starts from the inner levels of professional identity and beliefs. The inner levels, in fact, strongly affect the outer levels of competencies and behaviour. These, in turn, influence and are influenced by the environment. By moving in this direction, I had empowered teachers in expanding their professional development on the basis of internal learning. This skill would assist them long after the teacher research project was over.

2. The process of moving from the inner to the outer levels of self-inquiry changes the teacher educator's role. Initially, at the inner level, I actively led the teacher researchers towards self-inquiry, whereas at outer levels, they led their own actions more autonomously, taking responsibility for their decisions and only occasionally seeking my advice.

3. The pattern of inquiry I helped teachers implement changed their superficial research practice. Initially, teachers sought, through AR, rapid solutions to their practical problems without attempting to shed light on underlying issues. This type of inquiry is neither systematic nor

Table 2. The Professional Development Pattern Underlying the AR Tools

AR Tool Sequencing	Self-Inquiry Levels
Personal logs	Ongoing reflective process
Perception questionnaires	Professional identity and beliefs
Teachers' open-ended/closed questionnaires	Competencies
Learners' open-ended/closed questionnaires	Mirroring competencies
COLT observation grids	Behaviour
Teachers' lesson recall sheets	Environment
Learners' lesson feedback sheets	Mirroring environment

developmental. Over time, though, teachers came to appreciate the value and benefits of longer-term inquiry focusing not on quick solutions but deeper understanding and thoughtful action.

During this phase of review and evaluation I also reflected on alternative approaches to sequencing the presentation and implementation of the AR tools and how those approaches would have altered teachers' inquiries. My reflections on these issues helped me understand the following:

- If I had not strongly encouraged the use of personal logs, I would not have supported teachers in developing self-awareness of the ongoing process, leading them from intrapersonal inquiry to interpersonal reflection.

- If closed questionnaires had been introduced before the open-ended ones, induced reflection would have interfered with teachers' spontaneous self-reflection.

- If learners' questionnaires and feedback sheets had been administered before the teachers' recall sheets, teachers' data would have probably been affected by learners' outcomes.

- If classroom observation had preceded teachers' perception of professional qualities of the external world, a judgmental stance towards deficiencies would have more likely occurred.

- If the national and local research studies had been carried out separately, the CEF-standardised test results for each language competency area would not have offered the teachers the chance to use such data to practically pose AR problems related to their classrooms and to gain a holistic view of the European objectives of the project.

Reflection

The normative approach of the RIC-CO project challenged me to engage in self-inquiry into the meaning and use of prescribed AR tools to support teacher researchers. The results of my inquiry led me to understand that the development of a holistic AR methodology is fostered by consistent use of the AR tools available. In particular, I gained an understanding of how the AR tools could be employed to exploit different levels of self-inquiry, moving from the inner to the outer levels to overcome teachers' habit of superficial research practice.

During different phases of my work with teachers, my role changed significantly. Initially, I facilitated the AR process by making decisions, planning reflective process actions, and taking the lead to assist the group by adjusting to their needs and research objectives. Subsequently, I collaborated with the group in negotiating and making decisions and suitable choices. I then participated in the AR process with my action of self-disclosure, sharing doubts and uncertainties. Finally, I advised the teachers as they gradually led their own self-inquiry actions.

Following this self-inquiry, I decided to take further reflective action by inviting the AR group to pursue practice as inquiry beyond the RIC-CO project. Subsequently, the teacher researchers supported their traditional peers in doing AR within the local TESOL-Italy group. In coordinating this event and thus continuing to engage in self-education, I learned that the AR group members modified their modus operandi in small but professionally significant ways when engaged with their peers. In pairs, they coherently planned and introduced the AR tools, emphasising the can-do learner-centred approach suggested by the CEF and thus showing increasing professional growth. The 25 potential teacher researchers who participated in the local AR benefited from the bottom-up approach in terms of peer empathy and professional competence. Moreover, I found that the practice of supporting the AR group in conducting teacher education was a source of personal professional renewal, deriving from the multiplying effect of the local action of the institutional RIC-CO project.

Further qualitative European research is currently in progress as a result of local project findings on the discrepancy of expected CEF outcomes. Local data indicated that although primary learners easily attained CEF A2 level, there is a mismatch between secondary learners' language competencies and the expected CEF B1/B2 levels.

My professional understanding will further benefit from guiding the group in investigating such issues and in seeking action which attempts to ensure pedagogical continuity between the different Italian educational levels. The starting point for this follow-up research is based on the recognition that pedagogical continuity between one level and another can be fostered when local actions are reflectively calibrated to "agreed common reference standards, purely descriptive in nature" (Trim, 2001, p. 5), such as the CEF standards.

Anna Franca Plastina teaches at the University of Calabria, Italy.

Note

1. ALTE is an association of institutions within Europe, each of which produces examinations and certification for language learners. Each member provides examinations of the language which is spoken as a mother tongue in that country or region.

CHAPTER 9

Sharing a Journey Towards Success: The Impact of Collaborative Study Groups and CALL in a Legal Context (*Italy*)

Alison Riley and Patricia Sours

Issue

The setting for our research was the law faculty of an eminent Italian university with a strong European heritage. This modern faculty is strongly oriented towards Europe, which was reflected in its decision to actively foster specialised language learning for all its undergraduates, offering courses in legal English, German, or French. The setting was thus supportive of specialised language teaching and also proved responsive to teachers' ideas for innovation and change. The research issue, however, was linked to two problematic factors beyond the teachers' control: a large, heterogeneous class and the flexibility that characterises the Italian university system. With legal language now a compulsory subject at the faculty, there were about 300 potential students per year for the 30-hour Legal English course. Our varied experience teaching university classes in Italy led us to expect that many students would never attend classes or sit the exam and that many who attended might drop out of the large class, with corresponding failure to complete the course and exam successfully.

In this challenging context, the issue calling most urgently for solution emerged as the following research question: How would it be possible in a large mixed-ability English for specific purposes (ESP) class to support the learning of all students (weaker, mid-range, and stronger) to ensure that all course participants managed to achieve the course objectives? This question fully addressed our concern that many students might fail to achieve their potential and complete the Legal English course and exam successfully.

The issue facing us was complex and seemed to call for a multifaceted approach. We decided to use a set of support systems to try to enhance students' motivation and autonomy and to investigate how these systems responded to the research question. The chief support systems were Patricia Sours's supplementary course, which was closely linked to Alison Riley's main course and specifically designed to support linguistically weaker students; supportive study groups to facilitate communicative opportunities, learner cooperation, and motivation to complete the course; adjustments to specially written course materials; and greater focus on a researched legal terminology project supported by computer-assisted language learning (CALL) opportunities facilitated by Sours.

THE ESP SYLLABUS

The students' prime common denominator was their shared interest in law, and the strongly content-based ESP syllabus was intended to provide a challenging and motivating course that would be useful during participants' university careers and in their future professional lives. Teaching was centred on authentic, unmodified texts (Johns, 1994), and thematically based language learning was promoted by focusing on meaning and use of language in key branches of the law. Our goal was to provide the stimulus and conditions in the classroom for learning based on a core legal language syllabus. There were two main course aims: (1) to acquire the knowledge and skills needed to understand authentic legal texts in English and (2) to acquire knowledge and understanding of basic legal terminology, together with the ability to research and consolidate specialised legal vocabulary using appropriate reference sources and methods. Further, we aimed to develop independent language strategies and skills in the legal English field in response to European legal professionals' growing need to interact in a multilingual legal community.

Background Literature

Adapting and individualising learner needs in any language program has for some time been demonstrated to be beneficial to learners (Altman & James, 1980; Harlow, 1987). By careful selection of a program of study that reflects the learner's internal syllabus (personal goals, motivation, learning preferences, and cognitive style) and the external syllabus (the academic and cultural context), instructors can work to create a curriculum that reflects these individual needs (O'Malley & Chamot, 1990; Oxford, 1990, 1997).

Convinced from practical experience as teachers and by research that communicative teaching methodology (Brumfit, 1984), collaborative group work (e.g., Oxford, 1997), and autonomous self-regulatory learning (Nunan, 1988; van Lier, 1996) have positive effects on the language learning classroom, we set about collecting data to investigate the impact of our syllabus on the students' perceptions of what was useful for them.

We felt that the usefulness of the solutions we chose to implement in the syllabus were directly linked to theories of motivation—yet which motivation theory? Dörnyei (2003) so rightly stated that motivation should be viewed as a multifaceted construct. Over the past four decades there has been a wide range of theories and research in social psychology (Gardner, 1985) and cognitive motivation (self-determination, attribution, and goal theories). In this study, we are primarily interested in discussing Deci and Ryan's (1985) self-determination theory. It was influential in our work and seemed to have the most relevance in our learning context. In particular, the theory applied to the solutions that we implemented into the syllabus over the course of 2 years to individualise the curriculum for large, heterogeneous classes. This self-determination theory addresses the "energizing of behavior" (Deci, Pelletier, Ryan, & Vallerand, 1991, pp. 325–326) as well as the direction issue—desired goals and outcomes. Deci et al. described humans as having certain basic and psychological needs, such as the need for competence, relatedness, and autonomy (or self-determination). They defined more clearly these needs as follows:

> Competence involves understanding how to attain various external and internal outcomes and being efficacious in performing the requisite actions; relatedness involves developing secure and satisfying connections with others in one's social milieu; and autonomy refers to being self-regulating of one's own actions. (Deci et al., 1991, p. 327)

Further studies have indicated that tangible manifestations of motivation are observable by the intensity of engagement, the attention to the task, the effort and the persistence to the effort (Crookes & Schmidt, 1991; van Lier, 1996), and receptivity (Allwright & Bailey, 1991). Researchers have found that less observable manifestations of motivation have to do with "personal goals, emotional arousal, personal agency beliefs" (Ford, 1992, p. 3), and intentional behaviour (Deci et al., 1991). We felt that all of these components were interacting with one another as we strove to understand their impact on motivation in our classroom setting.

For example, we tried to be as attentive as possible to students' intrinsic needs as described in the self-determination theory. Because the course had been set up to be informative in terms of access to resources and supportive (with supplementary courses offered), we felt that students were well aware of how to acquire the competence for requisite outcomes. In addition, the organisation of study groups within the larger classroom setting offered them the opportunity to collaborate and interact in a nonthreatening manner (relatedness) with fellow students. It was now up to the students to make conscious choices and self-regulate their learning options.

Because the syllabus offered opportunities in the classroom (the contextual conditions) to satisfy the needs described in the self-determination theory, we were curious about which choices the students would make. At the same time, we were attentive observers in this process as we gauged students' personal investments (e.g., effort, intensity of engagement, interest) in the learning process. We intended for the various instruments used in this research project to help us discover if the support systems we had created were providing what the students needed to fulfil the course objectives and feel confident enough to sit for the exam. However, it proved difficult to pinpoint exactly which of the elements of the syllabus offered the most support. All of these processes were in "continuous and interdependent movement" (van Lier, 1996, p. 65) within the classroom.

Procedures

ACTION RESEARCH

Having identified our issue and gathered a knowledge base to lead us forwards, we moved to step three of Strickland's (1988) model of action research: planning an action. The early stages of our collaborative work consisted of regular discussion, sharing of ideas and observations, individual thought, and further discussion. This enabled us to define the research question and set in place a series of instruments designed to collect the multiple forms of data we would need. We agreed that determination and focusing our energy were key factors: "Action research begins with a starting point for development within one's practice and having the will to invest energy in pursuing it" (Altrichter, Posch, & Somekh, 1993, p. 7).

Our chief investigative instruments into the contribution of the support systems are described in the sections that follow. For steps in the action research process and many of the instruments we used, Altrichter et al. (1993) provided a wealth of ideas and practical advice in their book *Teachers Investigate Their Work*, which we drew on widely.

Start-of-course questionnaires. Students completed these in the first week of lessons. They provided us with valuable information regarding their language learning experiences over the years, learning style preferences, and personal objectives in relation to the course. This information helped us personalise our relationships with students. We asked students to respond to closed questions (e.g., What other languages have you studied and for how long?); open-ended questions (e.g., Can you think of any particular language learning methods that you personally have used with success in the past?); and a Likert scale from 1 to

6 regarding how proficient they were in English language skills (listening, speaking, reading, writing, and pronunciation).

Midcourse progress report. This report (see Appendix A) used open and closed questions and acted as our thermometer for changes in real time. We created this tool to check students' understanding and progress in such a large heterogeneous class, with questions such as "Can you understand the teacher most of the time?" or "Are you working regularly on your legal terminology system?" The report was designed to encourage students to think about their learning and exchange experiences and advice with their peers. One copy was completed by each study group.

End-of-course assessment. This assessment (see Appendix B) was administered during one of the last lessons. It was designed to provide concrete evidence for reflections on the impact of our support systems, suggesting possible changes to be incorporated into the following year's course. Students quickly assessed the value of a full range of course features and components, rating on a scale of 1 to 7 the extent to which a specific support system was useful. Further open-ended questions gave students scope to express full personal evaluations, providing confirmation of procedures or suggesting the need for adjustments.

Charts. These contained key data for collecting and assessing students' results and were created from the enrolment register of students' names and modified as more data on attendance, exam attempts, and results were collected. They proved to be invaluable instruments in our research. The class attendance and results chart, compiled using a simple table format in Microsoft Word, was easy to convert into a specific study group chart to visualise results of students in the same study group, enabling observations to be made.

Student interviews. After the end of the course, we conducted interviews with individual volunteers, asking for explanations of personal responses, a possibility not provided by questionnaires. Interviews were held in a friendly, informal style in the interviewee's preferred language, generally English. Interviews were unstructured, allowing interviewees to develop their personal concerns in their answers (Altrichter et al., 1993) and enabling us to investigate more fully. Questions from the end-of-course assessment were used as convenient cues for the interview, and the interviewer took brief notes.

In addition, data were collected through a research diary kept by one of us and ongoing collaborative discussion between both of us throughout the project. All data were collected over 2 years, and these are referred to as Year 1 and Year 2.

SUPPORT SYSTEMS

We implemented three kinds of support systems for this study: study groups, a supplementary course, and computer research sessions.

Study groups. Study groups of three to five students were formed to work together in the larger class context throughout the Legal English course. These groups had a dual function:

1. They gave group members a continuing forum to provide mutual support during the course, encouraging and facilitating active participation of all group members towards successful course completion. For example, at the beginning of the week, group members would review and compare homework activities, discuss problems, and update absentees.

2. They served as convenient, ready-made units for communicative activities in the larger class setting, including valuable oral practice for the exam. For example, a jigsaw reading activity on an authentic legal text with focus on meaning and language could be followed up by a teacher-led discussion to highlight main points and clarify problematic areas.

Groups were set up in the first week of the Legal English course. The teachers explained the twin purposes of the groups clearly in English and Italian; then students were instructed to form groups of three, four, or five. Students formed groups on the basis of friendships, study partnerships, or seating arrangements in class that day (there was little room for manoeuvre in the crowded classroom). Study groups were instructed to use English for interactive language activities. However, we recognised that with a shared first language, students were likely to code switch into Italian for organisational activities within the group (Hancock, 1997). We decided not to interfere with language choice for these activities, because it was likely that at lower language levels, at least, a group's function as a forum for mutual support could well be achieved more efficiently in the students' native tongue.

Supplementary course. We decided that students who were linguistically weaker (often the silent members of the study groups) in our mixed-proficiency setting needed an opportunity to engage in relevant interactive language activities outside the larger classroom experience. The start-of-course questionnaires revealed that many students felt they needed more practice developing their listening and speaking skills, even though the majority of them had studied English for at least 5 years in secondary school. As a result, the main course objective for the supplementary course was to improve students' communicative competence. Students attended 2 hours per week for 10 weeks, and teachers encouraged active participation in the lessons. The tasks organised for completion during class hours reflected our pedagogic approach to the learning process: collaborative group work (e.g., use of jigsaw reading), explicit instruction in listening and reading comprehension strategies, and suggestions for further linguistic practice through the use of the Internet. The legal texts used were generally on the same themes as the regular Legal English class.

Computer research sessions. Research sessions took place in a computer lab with two students per computer (which encouraged collaboration), with a maximum of 18 students per session. The start-of-course questionnaire completed in the first week of class showed that many students in the law faculty did not have much expertise using the computer other than for e-mail. In response, the course initially concentrated on giving them basic computer and research skills. We reviewed word-processing skills, online dictionary use (general dictionaries, legal dictionaries, and multilingual dictionaries, which included translation of legal texts), and important sites for research (e.g., the European Union official site). The second part of the course was specific to students' research in the completion of the required terminology projects: definitions, related words, collocation, and legal words in context.

Results

Our results for the impact of the three support systems are reviewed in this section.

Study groups. Using the full set of instruments previously described, our precise concern for this part of the research was to investigate whether students in a large, heterogeneous ESP class could be supported in successful course completion by specially created study groups, designed to act as regular working units throughout the course to provide support and communicative opportunities.

In reviewing group members' performance for Year 2, we found that a minority of students were not assigned to a known study group. These students might have floated from group to group, attended irregularly, or simply been absent during the early phase of the course, when study group membership was recorded. The results showed that 31% of students not assigned to a study group dropped out of the course. Yet only 10% of the students assigned to a group did so, thus 90% of the students who joined a study group completed the Legal English course. These figures suggest that study group membership contributed to course completion. But did these students go on to achieve course objectives, demonstrated by passing the exam? Sixty-two percent of students assigned to study groups went on to pass the exam; by contrast, the exam success rate for students not assigned to study groups was only 54%. Thus it would seem that study group membership was a factor linked to successful achievement of objectives. Although we were disappointed that 38% of study group members (most of whom regularly attended class) did not sit for the exam despite all the support systems, the results suggest that study groups seem to make a positive difference.

The exam results for members of specific study groups showed that some groups achieved a high success rate. In more than one third of the study groups (11 out of 28) all members passed, many with flying colours. However, there were four groups from which no members attempted the exam. In the remaining 13 groups, success rates varied and no significant patterns emerged; these were mainly the larger groups of four or five students. It was interesting to speculate whether the highly successful groups were also the ones in which students appreciated and made the most of practice and support activities in their groups. The questionnaires revealed mixed responses to study groups. Some individuals specified that study group activities were beneficial and that membership encouraged them to complete the course, and yet others judged the groups useless and a waste of time. Comments in the Midcourse Progress Report (performed in study groups) were predominantly positive. For "Which activities do you find most useful?" a high proportion of groups replied "Working in the study group." One group (Year 2) summarised members' satisfaction this way:

> We have found the course very useful in the approach to the study of the language. We think so because the teacher has led students to start many discussions, so making them able to use English language as a form to communicate and not to consider it a mere subject of study.

These indicators seem to support the benefits of using study groups.

Supplementary course and computer research sessions. Because two new support courses had been added to the program—a supplementary course and computer research sessions—we were curious to find out if they had had an impact on our research issue. Were all the students in our large, heterogeneous setting (weaker, midrange, and stronger proficiencies) benefiting from these additions, thus empowering them to confidently sit for the exam and successfully fulfil the course objectives? This section focuses on the data collected over the course of 2 academic years from three of our research instruments: the start-of-course questionnaires, the end-of-course assessment questionnaires, and the class attendance and results chart. The findings revealed through these instruments proved useful not only by setting in motion structural changes in our courses from year to year, but also by initiating changes in our pedagogic approach to the original syllabus.

A close examination of the class attendance and results chart of Year 1 revealed that enrolment in the supplementary course had been relatively low and with irregular attendance (the class began with 25 students and finished with 12). Based on the results of this instrument, we decided in Year 2 to introduce a pretest entitled "How's Your English?" on the first day of the Legal English class. The pretest would give students an opportunity to determine their current linguistic competence. In this way, students would be able to determine their own needs and judge whether or not to participate in the support programs offered, in particular the extra class hours for the supplementary course. Of the 101 students who took the pretest, 35% attained a score below the minimum level required for the Legal English course.

In contrast to Year 1, 38 students in Year 2 enrolled in and consistently attended the supplementary course. We were curious who these students were. We gathered the statistics from our class attendance and results chart and discovered some interesting results. Of the 38 students, 17 had attained low scores on the pretest (approximately half of the low-level students decided to attend the class), 15 had attained high scores (showing impressive motivation), and 6 had not taken the pretest yet decided to attend the extra course.

We also changed our pedagogic approach to give students more responsibility in the organisation of their learning. The need for that change became obvious in Year 1 when long lines of students requested consultation during office hours every week. Students were concerned about the terminology project, which was a required and critical component in the final assessment for the course.

At the end of Year 1, we reviewed the computer research sessions, which had been started in Year 1 to instruct students on how to use the Internet for legal language research purposes. The class was organised in 2-hour weekly sessions for 4 weeks. Once again, reviewing the class attendance and results chart at the end of Year 1, we discovered that the turnout had been low and inconsistent. Yet in the end-of-course assessment questionnaire (Year 1), responses indicated that students had valued the computer research sessions. For example, 11 of 20 student questionnaires had rated its usefulness at 6 (a very high grade on the scale). Nevertheless, attendance had been sporadic, which perhaps related more to the amount of class time required than to any lack of interest.

We subsequently took a number of steps to address this situation. First, in Year 2 we shortened the computer research sessions by concentrating them into 4 hours instead of 8, thereby creating the possibility for more students to attend the course. Second, we decided to allocate more credit to the terminology project as part of the oral exam grade. Finally, on the first day of regular class we explicitly encouraged students to sign up for the supplementary computer course.

Not surprisingly, after looking over the class attendance and results chart (Year 2), it emerged that all 38 supplementary course students had attended the computer research sessions, and 10 attendees from the Legal English course had chosen to enrol only in the computer research sessions course. This increased the total to 48 students (or 48% of those attending the main course) opting for some form of support system in addition to their regular class. In the end, 75% of the students who participated in the supplementary course and computer research sessions course sat for the exam. Another rather unexpected result emerging from the class attendance and results chart was that the final evaluations for the terminology projects and the final marks for Legal English were higher for students who had also attended the support courses. The quality of the terminology projects was superior. In fact, 78% of the attending students who sat for the exam sessions received an "excellent" or a "very good" rating on their terminology projects. In the final evaluation, the terminology project rating (excellent, very good, good, fair, pass) was figured into the mark attained in the oral exam, so it had a direct effect on learner outcomes. Of the 36 attendees who sat for the exam, 56% got "excellent" as the final evaluation. We found that the research instruments provided data that positively supported our research question.

Furthermore, the end-of-course assessment questionnaire revealed that the general quality of all of the students' terminology projects had improved from Year 1. For example, question 5 in the end-of-course assessment inquired, "If you consider one thing that helped you learn the most in the course, what would you say?" Even though this was an open-ended question, many students wrote the same things. In fact, the terminology project was rated third after class materials and teacher explanations by many students. Based on student input on what they valued, this was confirmation for us that students appreciated the terminology project for its relevancy and the learning experience it provided. In the Midcourse Progress Report (Year 2), one group said, "The terminology project helps us to reach and understand new legal words and lessons."

In spite of these positive indications, we are convinced that the students' success not only was due to attendance in these supplementary courses, but also was enhanced by the interdependence of all the different processes working together throughout the semester. This was clearly evidenced in the end-of-course assessment for Year 2, when students indicated what had been useful for them in the course organisation and methodology section (see Appendix B). Students rated the usefulness of different parts of the syllabus using a Likert scale from 1 to 7, with 1 indicating "low/the least" and 7 indicating "high/the most." Table 1 presents results for the three highest ratings (5, 6, and 7). Sixty-four questionnaires were handed in, 32 of which were from participants in the

Table 1. Students' Rating of Course Elements

Course Organisation and Methodology	Student Evaluation			Total n	% of 64/32
	5	6	7		
Course description	18	15	10	43/64	67
Course materials	8	26	20	54/64	84
Book: *English for Law* (Riley, 1991)	17	27	6	50/64	78
Belonging to study groups	14	9	7	30/64	46
Communicative activities in study groups	10	15	5	30/64	46
Supplementary course	7	11	8	26/32	81
Computer research sessions	6	8	11	25/32	78

supplementary course and computer research sessions. The last two columns indicate the combined number of students who circled 5, 6, or 7, in relation to the total number of questionnaires submitted.

Table 1 confirms that, on the whole, students rated quite favourably the course organisation and methodology that we had proposed. Specially written class materials were the most highly valued, at 84% (this was consistent with the questionnaire input from Year 1, in which 82 of the 84 questionnaires, or 98%, rated them 5, 6, or 7). The supplementary courses were also considered favourably. The study groups and the communicative activities had the lowest overall ratings, yet nonetheless at least 46% of the students considered them useful.

Reflection

Our action research instruments enabled us to capture what the students considered important in our specific classroom setting and gave us as teachers much-needed input for shaping the direction of future courses. We were able to examine our ongoing efforts from year to year and then adapt in response to the students' needs.

In this chapter we have focused on just three support systems. The data we collected provided the tangible means for us to observe these systems and make changes to them. Yet we discovered that it was only through our ongoing dialogic discussions that we were able to make any sense out of our investigative efforts. We found that we needed to go beyond the data as we attempted to glean perceptions of quality or success in students' efforts, their engagement with and commitment to the task, and their assuming of responsibility for their own learning. As the decision makers in the pedagogical process, we had implemented changes throughout the 2 years and had set up the conditions for change. Yet someone critically evaluating the data only would not see radical changes.

As teachers we tried to be responsive to the ever-changing, dynamic process of language learning. Van Lier (1996) described what he called quality of exposure, which is determined by "providing access in the form of comprehensibility, contextuality, familiarity, assistance, affective factors, and so on" (p. 53). In this ESP course, we strove towards this quality of exposure to legal language through a syllabus that was designed to offer the students many choices: It was left up to the students to become responsible for which choices to make through personal reasoned decisions in order to achieve positive outcomes. Turning to the self-determination theory of Deci and Ryan (1985), we attempted to energise student behaviour so that we could make an effect on desired goals and outcomes.

Our personal appraisal of the research, backed up by diary entries, strongly indicates that a vital element of the project was collaborative research between the two teachers involved, acting on an equal footing. Our collaboration involved sharing experiences and discussing outcomes. However, the focus of the research was different for each of us, fitting the model of collaborative research described by Altrichter et al. (1993). The nature of our research presupposed a willingness to change and be flexible, which meant that we were always putting ourselves on the line as teachers. This was a risky strategy, and we benefited from professional and moral support from one another. Although the importance of collegial collaboration is not exactly an original discovery, firsthand accounts can convey the immediacy of the experience and be inspirational:

> Do not just believe it. Experience it. What is the point of simply knowing it? Do it. (Edge, 2001, p. 9)

That is a message we hope also shines through from our experience.

Alison Riley teaches at the law faculties of Ferrara and Padua Universities, Italy.[1]
Patricia Sours teaches at the University of Padua and at the University of Ferrara, Italy.[2]

Note

1. Alison Riley wrote the following sections: Issue; Procedures—Action Research, and Action Research—student interviews, and research diary; Procedures—Support Systems—Study Groups; Results—Study Groups; and Reflection—action research.

2. Patricia Sours wrote the following sections: Background Literature; Procedures—Action Research—start-of-course questionnaires, the midcourse progress report, the end-of-course assessment, charts, and collaborative discussion; Procedures—Support Systems—Supplementary Course, and Computer Research Sessions; Results—Supplementary Course and Computer Research Sessions; and Reflection—motivation.

Appendix A: Midcourse Progress Report

Work together in your STUDY GROUP and discuss the progress you are making on the Legal English course so far. Your discussion may include the following aspects:

A) LESSONS

- Can you understand the teacher most of the time?

- Is the language level of lessons about right for you (or too easy/hard)?

- Which activities do you find most useful?
- Would you like to request any changes in approach or activities?

B) COURSE CONTENT

- Do you understand the main course content so far?
- What type of materials (*course materials, slides*) have you found useful during lessons?
- What is your response to the specialised language component of the course?

C) INDIVIDUAL STUDY

- What work have you succeeded in doing each week?
- Are you experiencing any difficulties?
- What materials (*course materials, book, dictionaries*) have you found useful for your individual studies?
- Are you working regularly on your legal terminology system?
- What practical study ideas would you like to share with other group members?

D) INTEGRATED ACTIVITIES

- If you are attending the Supplementary Course discuss its usefulness in relation to the *Lingua giuridica inglese* course.
- If you have attended a computer lab session for terminology project work, discuss its usefulness.
- Would you recommend these activities to other group members?

E) EXAMS

- Is the format of the Legal English exam clear?
- Do you feel you are working positively towards the exam?
- Would you like opportunities for specific practice before the exam?
- Discuss how and when you intend to prepare for the exam. Can the study group help?
- Have you got any questions about the exam?

— — — — — — — — — — — — — — — — — — — —

Please write your most important conclusions and requests directly beside the questions or in the space below:

Appendix B: End-of-Course Assessment, May 2005

The following information will help us in our research. We will use your answers to evaluate this year's course and consider improvements for the future. The information you give will NOT be used to evaluate you as a student. Thank you! We appreciate your cooperation.

Corso di Laurea

PLEASE GIVE YOUR HONEST RESPONSE BY CIRCLING THE APPROPRIATE NUMBER.

   (1 = low/the least, 7 = high/the most, NA = not applicable)

1) COURSE ORGANISATION & METHODOLOGY

How useful were the following for you?

Course description (programma)	1	2	3	4	5	6	7	NA
Course materials (dispensa)	1	2	3	4	5	6	7	NA
English for Law book	1	2	3	4	5	6	7	NA
Teacher's explanations in class	1	2	3	4	5	6	7	NA
Belonging to a study group	1	2	3	4	5	6	7	NA
Communicative activities in study groups	1	2	3	4	5	6	7	NA
Individual consultation (ricevimento studenti)	1	2	3	4	5	6	7	NA
Guest lecture by an English jurist	1	2	3	4	5	6	7	NA
Supplementary course	1	2	3	4	5	6	7	NA
Computer lab sessions for terminology projects	1	2	3	4	5	6	7	NA

If you participated in the *Supplementary Course*, how useful were the following?

Conversation in pairs/small groups	1	2	3	4	5	6	7	NA
Pronunciation lessons and practice	1	2	3	4	5	6	7	NA
Jigsaw for fluency and comprehension	1	2	3	4	5	6	7	NA
Teacher's explanations in class	1	2	3	4	5	6	7	NA
Computer sessions	1	2	3	4	5	6	7	NA

[Questions 2, 3, 4, 9, and 10 omitted]

5) If you could choose <u>one thing</u> that helped you learn the most in the course, what would you say?

6) What would you change about this course if you had the chance to do it again? What would you add? What would you delete?

7) Which of your objectives have you satisfied by following this course?

8) Name 3 things that have encouraged you to complete the course.

Thank you!

P.S. Would you be willing to take part in a brief interview with your teacher about your experience on the course? If so, please leave an e-mail address where we may contact you to arrange an appointment.

CHAPTER 10

Aspects of Teacher-Generated Language in the Language Classroom (*UK*)

Linda Taylor

Issue

The research reported in this chapter arises directly from my work as a language teacher and teacher educator in Britain, where I have witnessed a significant change in emphasis from teaching to learning (e.g., Larsen-Freeman, 2000). This gradual shift has been away from a teacher-centred methodology, often referred to as *transmission* style, towards an *interpretation* one, in which learning is managed and facilitated through pair and group work (Barnes, 1976; Wright, 1987). As a result, I have become increasingly aware of the importance of variety in classroom interaction patterns and of clarity in the language that teachers use for the management of learning. These are crucial factors when training novice teachers to teach English, through the medium of English, to multilingual classes. The special nature of language in language teaching has been acknowledged by Roberts (1998), who categorised it in three ways: (1) as a medium for transmitting information, (2) as a system of rules, and (3) as a social experience played out in the classroom.

This chapter focuses on the aspect of a language teacher's competence that has been referred to variously as *teacher talk* (Bailey, 2001), *classroom language* (Spratt, 1994), or *teacher-generated classroom language* (Winn-Smith, 2001). This type of teacher talk fulfils a number of functions, including what one might readily associate with teaching, such as presenting and practising new language, explaining meaning, providing models, or correcting errors. However, it has other important functions, such as organising classroom layout, giving instructions, providing encouragement, forming groups, maintaining discipline, or personalising content. Much of this language is heard only in classrooms and may not necessarily come naturally to teachers.

The impetus for the action research reported in this chapter arose from difficulties that one of my novice teacher colleagues (henceforth "Colin") had with managing teacher-independent tasks for language learning. On hearing his plea, "If you just tell me the rules, I'll follow them," I was embarrassed to admit that I had no rules to give. Until that time, I had not thought of a language class in terms of applying a set of rules to be followed. I had thought of it rather as a purposeful interaction in which learning takes place. In order to help Colin, I had to shift my frame of reference, to observe and document my own and other teachers' relevant practices, with the aim of creating a set of so-called rules that might be useful for Colin and others like him. I decided to carry out research in the context that Colin and I are typically involved with, that is, classes of adult students of English for general purposes. My intention was to investigate the spoken language generated by teachers in their language classes. Therefore, I set for myself the following question: With specific reference to setting up teacher-independent tasks for language learning, in what ways do I and other teachers use language to manage learning, relate to individuals, and foster interaction in the language classroom?

Background Literature

TEACHER ROLE, CLASSROOM INTERACTION, AND CLASSROOM DISCOURSE

In British educational contexts, students in classes have been described as "interactive learning communities" rather than a "captive audience for instruction" (Britton, 1994, p. 263). In this climate, it is becoming clear that much more than teaching goes on in language classrooms. There has been a corresponding evolution in teacher-student discourse since Sinclair and Coulthard (1975) produced their seminal exchange structure model. This model presented a lesson as a series of transactions, consisting of boundary exchanges and teaching exchanges. The boundary exchange framed and focussed the upcoming teaching exchange, for example, by the use of discourse markers, such as "well . . . now. . . ." The teaching exchange then typically comprised an opening move from the teacher, followed by an answering move from the student, and then a follow-up move from the teacher, as in Figure 1.

The introduction of periods of teacher-independent group and pair work into language lessons has led to more varied classroom interaction patterns, along

```
(T = teacher, P = any pupil who speaks)
  T: ... What's that, what is it?
  P: Saw.
  T: It's a saw, yes this is a saw ...
```

Source: From Sinclair and Coulthard (1975, pp. 93–94)

Figure 1. Example teaching exchange in the exchange structure model.

a cline from teacher-led to student-initiated interaction. Ellis (2003) refers to interaction patterns as participatory structures, ranging from private speech to small group interaction. In the context of setting up tasks, I am concerned here with the social participatory structure, in which the teacher speaks to the whole class.

Developments in classroom interactions reflect the link between language functions and speaker roles. For teachers, these may include those of conversation partner, working group member, chairperson, source, guide or facilitator, along with more traditional roles (Corden, 1992). In recent studies of classroom discourse, Walsh (2003) worked to discover relationships between teacher talk and teaching objectives, and Oliver and Mackey (2003) classified teacher-learner exchanges in language classes according to whether they focused on content, explicit language, communication, or management. My research addresses classroom management issues as well as aspects of classroom communication that are social in character.

THE USE OF TASKS IN LANGUAGE TEACHING

Littlejohn (1996) discusses the importance of tasks in fostering communication and serving as an interface between the teacher and students. There is a substantial body of research on tasks in the field of language teaching and learning, and the notion of *task* itself has widely varying interpretations in the literature (Bygate, Skehan, & Swain, 2001; Ellis, 2003). Tasks in language teaching are typically staged in three phases (e.g., Willis, 1996): (1) a pretask phase devoted to setting up the task, (2) an in-task phase in which students perform the task, and (3) a posttask phase devoted to feedback and possible follow-up work. The classes in my case study used the *Cutting Edge* (e.g., Cunningham & Moor, 1998) series of English language textbooks, which emphasise tasks and define them as "oral or written activity, in which the primary goal is to achieve a particular outcome or product" (p. 4). Much of the literature explores the relationship between tasks and language output from students. Less attention has been paid to language output from teachers, and few studies have been set in intact classes (Samuda, 2001). This chapter is concerned solely with teacher-generated language, and deals with entire classes rather than short classroom extracts.

TEACHER-GENERATED LANGUAGE AND THE TEACHER-LEARNER RELATIONSHIP

Drawing on child language acquisition studies, researchers into second language acquisition have been interested in the way that a native speaker makes linguistic adjustments to a nonnative speaker's level. Long (1981, 1983) called attention to the beneficial role of interactional adjustments, such as repetition and checking of understanding. In addition, Chaudron (1988) provided a list of modifications which teachers in language classes tend to make to their normal speech patterns, including pausing and slowing the rate of speech. Meanwhile, the emotional or affective dimension of teaching, including its manifestation through teacher-generated language, has received increasing attention in the TESOL field (Arnold, 1999; Norman, 2003). The role of teacher-generated language in creating and maintaining rapport, or positive relationships within the classroom (Millrood, 2004), is one such dimension that has influenced the research reported here.

Procedures

SCOPE AND METHODS

As a preliminary to the larger study, I made an audio recording of one of my upper intermediate lessons and transcribed it. The lesson was based on five teacher-independent activities, and the following transcription represents my use of language from the beginning of the lesson until the end of the first such activity:

> [General chat as students settle down.] All right, so the topic for today then, we're on Session 7, and we've got a lot to get through, we're going to be looking at memos, voice mail, and e-mail. So we're going to listen to a telephone conversation, which is going to lead to a memo, and I want to show you the memo layout first of all, OK? [Passes around handouts, chatting to students, "Have you got one of these? You've got a bad cold? It's winter time now. Good job we're not living in Scotland, you'd be even colder."] OK, so on our Session 7 you've got a couple of tasks here, so have you got those tasks for your handbook? There's Task A and Task B. The example says [reads rubric]. Now at the bottom of your handout you have an example of how someone has answered that question. So with the person sitting next to you [divides them into pairs]—two, two, two, two, two, two, two, two. So would you have a look at it, read the question and see what you think of it as an answer? You've got 3 minutes to have a look. So on the board there are the points that you had to include in the memo. So have a look at the memo and see if the writer has mentioned all the points in the answer. [Students work independently of the

teacher for the allotted time.] All right, so has he written to all the staff? Yes? All staff. So that's correct isn't it?

In the pilot lesson, I noted a relative lack of teacher-student interaction in the pretask portion, when I set up the first task. I also noticed that I structured the instructions by first setting the context for the place of the task in the lesson as a whole, and then using single word items, such as "so" and "now," to signal managing of behaviour and focusing of attention. I discovered that I used language interactively to create rapport at three points in the extract: when chatting generally to students before the lesson actually began, when giving out handouts, and when discussing the results of the task. These observations informed my thinking when I began my larger project.

The larger project was based on data from my own classes and from those of 12 novice teachers during an English language summer course at my institution. Through collecting these data my aim was to deepen my understanding of my own teaching as well as to develop my understanding of how I could better support novice teachers in my role as teacher educator. This research thus informed my professional practices on two levels.

The novice teachers who took part in my study were using students in our summer course for their supervised teaching practice whilst preparing for the Cambridge ESOL Certificate in English Language Teaching to Adults (CELTA) qualification. Their tutors, including me, were also teaching the same summer course classes. The data used for the study comprised audio recordings of classes taught by me and my novice teacher colleagues. Levels of language proficiency in these classes ranged from way-stage user to independent user (Council of Europe, 2001). Classes consisted of between 14 and 16 learners: natives of Brazil, China, Egypt, Iran, Italy, Japan, Korea, Mexico, and Saudi Arabia. The lessons ranged from 30 to 45 minutes in duration, and formed the basis for the Lessons from the Classroom Assignment requirement for CELTA assessment. Individual institutions that offer the CELTA scheme design their own assignment brief, and I used the following one in this study:

> Drawing on your own teaching experience and observation of tutors and peers, reflect on what you have learned about the relationship between classroom language, classroom management, and student output. For this assignment, make an audio recording of a teaching practice lesson or lessons. Write one to two pages of analysis of the lesson(s) and attach these as an appendix to your assignment.

I recorded entire lessons for my research and examined the transcribed data using discourse analysis and conversational analysis. Discourse analysis seeks to explain why a particular speaker utters particular words at a particular point in the unfolding communicative process. The main emphasis in a conversation analysis approach, on the other hand, is on how relationships are manifested through interaction. I combined these two approaches in my research, with the purpose of investigating the following in the context of entire lessons:

1. General issues of staging and interaction arising from the use of tasks

2. Issues specific to structural features of pretask, teacher-fronted stages

3. Issues specific to interactional features of pretask, teacher-fronted stages

The business of organising equipment to ensure effective, unobtrusive recording of teaching practice sessions was easily managed, because the teachers took responsibility for doing this as part of the preparations for their Lessons from the Classroom Assignment. I made my own recordings of the lessons I taught with the same classes. The recording equipment was in every instance placed next to the teacher on the front desk.

DATA ANALYSIS

In this section, I illustrate the steps I took in my analysis, using two examples from my data: an upper-intermediate lesson (henceforth Lesson A) and a lower-intermediate lesson (henceforth Lesson B). The first step in the research process was to transcribe whole lessons in order to contextualise the pretask stages within them. Initially, I made transcripts comprising teacher and student utterances, but in order to focus on teacher-generated language I edited the transcripts to show the teachers' words only (see Figure 2). When a student spoke, I

Hello everyone.
Did you have a nice weekend?
What did you do at the weekend, what did you do? (ST)
You went travelling. Where did you go? (ST)
Very nice. What did you think? (ST)
Yeah. Was the weather nice? (ST)
It didn't rain, (ST)
on Saturday. (ST)
Yeah. Did anybody feel the earthquake yesterday in Nottingham? (ST)(ST)
Yeah it wasn't very long. (ST) (ST)
Three point eight on the Richter Scale,
but it was about half past three in the afternoon. (ST)
Half past three. (ST)
Yeah the watch, yeah it went forward yesterday,
but apparently we haven't had an earthquake in Nottingham like that
for 250 years. (ST)

Figure 2. Rough transcription.

---

indicated the existence of a student turn on my transcript by the code (*ST*). This code denoted any student utterance recognisable as a word, phrase, or sentence, irrespective of purpose, and was used as a crude measure of how much interaction went on between students and teacher at each lesson stage.

I next made charts for each lesson, showing lesson stages and associated interaction patterns. I also listed how transitions from each lesson stage to the next were signalled (Tables 1 and 2 are the charts derived from Lesson A). From these charts, it was possible to identify teacher-fronted pretask extracts and to contextualise them within the staging and interaction which occurred during entire lessons. The charts allowed me to see how discourse markers signalled transitions from one stage to the next, and indicated the relevant importance of each upcoming stage.

I then went back to the transcripts and refined my transcription conventions, over several exposures to the audio recordings, during my detailed analysis (Table 3 represents the beginning of the lower-intermediate lesson, Lesson B). Through this coding process, I discovered that most of the language used for setting up tasks was managerial (shown in bold in Table 3), but there were elements used by the teachers to encourage or simulate interaction (italicised in

Table 1. Sequence of Stages and Interaction Patterns in Lesson A

Lesson Focus: Speaking Skills
(Communication task using leisure vocabulary and function of expressing preference)
Class Level: Upper intermediate
Class Duration: 35 minutes
Materials: three overhead projector slides, game cards, questionnaires, paper, and pens

Stage	Interaction
1. General chat	Student-class, teacher-class
2. Set up task	Teacher-class, student-class
3. Task–brainstorm vocabulary	Student-student group work
4. Feedback from task	Student-class, teacher-class
5. Sensitize to context/language for main task	Teacher-class, student-class
6. Set up main task	Teacher-class, student-class
7. Communication task	Student-student mingling
8. Feedback from main task	Student-class
9. Check language, understanding for next task	Teacher-class, student-class
10. Task-fill in questionnaire	Private, individual work
11. Take in questionnaires and close	Teacher-class, student-class

Table 2. Sequence of Discourse Markers Associated With Each Stage in Lesson A

Discourse Markers	Function
Hello . . .	Opening
But anyway I'm going to follow on a little bit . . .	Signalling start of lesson proper
OK so I'll put this . . .	Setting up first task
Shall we show it to the others	Signalling feedback
Right now . . .	Signalling new task
OK now what these are, these are . . .	Setting up new task
All right then	Signalling feedback
Right now this is for . . .	Signalling new task
Well do you want to . . .	Signalling change of plan
Now can you . . .	Setting up task in line with new plan
OK well . . .	Closing

Table 3), and there were instances when the teachers referred to shared knowledge (underscored in Table 3).

As a follow-up to my analysis, and as the final step in the research procedure, I conducted a workshop session with the novice teachers, whose insights gained from their audio recordings and from the process of drafting their Lessons From the Classroom assignments were discussed. The workshop focussed on setting up teacher-independent tasks for language learning. The brief for it follows:

> Based on your audio recorded lesson(s) and on your reading of the TESOL literature, have you developed any "rules" or "guidelines" of your own for giving instructions, e.g., when setting up tasks or beginning an exercise with your students? Take 5 minutes to think about this question, and write down ideas. We shall then share views and formulate guidelines together, based on your lessons and mine.

Results

PRELIMINARY ISSUES OF STAGING AND INTERACTION ARISING FROM THE USE OF TASKS

In terms of exchange structure, the data revealed a variety of interaction patterns. The significance of the warm-up stage of lessons in encouraging student-teacher interactions comes through clearly, and Lesson A (see Table 1) is an

Table 3. Revised Transcription Conventions in Lesson B

Order	Teacher-Fronted Interaction
1	Right, good morning everybody, we'll make a start.
2	cos [because] you have three teachers this morning, then Pete, so four altogether
3	*OK*
4	so we need to start now
5	*did you go to Cambridge at the weekend* (ST) *anybody else* (ST) *yeah* (ST)
6	you went to Cambridge
	(latecomer enters)
7	morning
8	**OK, first of all**
9	because it's Monday morning and we all feel a bit sleepy . . . tired
10	**I'd like you to come into the middle please . . . come into the middle here**
11	**everybody into here**
	(Students move)
12	**OK, just go round and talk to each other, and what you're going to find out is**
13	**what do you like most and least about England**
14	*OK*
15	**so talk to as many people in the group as you can**
16	*yeah*
17	**just for three minutes**
18	*yeah*
19	**just to each other**
	(Task begins)

Note: Transcription shows teacher's words only, divided into utterances. Language related to setting up tasks is in **bold** type; teacher questions or checks are in *italics*; personal and social references specific to the class are underscored; and student turns are indicated by (*ST*).

example of this. It starts with the typical sequence of moves: teacher opening, student answering, and teacher follow-up. However, the traditional sequence soon breaks down, as the teacher's controlling role is relinquished in favour of that of conversation partner; the discourse now continues with opening and answering roles reversed.

Lesson A had 11 stages, with three teacher-independent tasks. The full gamut of Ellis's (2003) individual and social participatory structures was used in this lesson. In the data overall, the number of tasks in a single lesson ranged from one to four, and the number of lesson stages ranged from 4 to 17. Although student turns could occur at any stage, there were fewest when tasks were set up. During instructions for tasks, there was in fact little student-teacher interaction, and a predominance of a one-way pattern, from teacher to student.

In terms of discourse markers linked to lesson staging, as in Lesson A (see Table 2), "well" signalled an unplanned shift of focus and also the lesson closing; "right" signalled a large, planned shift of focus; "all right then" signalled an important feedback stage; "now" signalled the setting up of an activity; and "OK" signalled the end of a stage or marked transition to the next stage. In the data overall, certain lexical items were recognisable as having either macro or micro functions in this way, in the context of entire lessons. Macromarkers signalled transition from one lesson stage to the next; micromarkers were used for further divisions within a stage. For example, task-specific instructions were signalled by "now," "if," "so," "em" (or "er"), and "just" (as shown in Table 3, Lesson B uses "so" and "just" as micromarkers).

STRUCTURAL FEATURES OF PRETASK, TEACHER-FRONTED LESSON STAGES

During the dedicated workshop on instruction giving, the novice teachers volunteered general ideas such as the following:

- For context setting —"Do the first few items with the class."

- For focusing concentration—"Get attention."

- For checking understanding—"Get a student to repeat back to you."

- For clear staging—"Sequence instructions clearly and set a time limit."

From their own lessons, they positively evaluated clear organisation, such as "explaining how many things [students] need to do," and they congratulated themselves if they managed grouping well. They acknowledged the negative impact of not being clear in their own minds about what they wanted students to do; not using examples; "getting instructions mixed up" with other work; and giving too many instructions at once. The full taxonomy of those structural rules that we drew up during the workshop discussion are as follows:

1. Frame the tasks and focus attention—"OK," "right," "all right"

2. Point backwards in time to set context—"We were doing this with Rosie yesterday"

3. Point forwards in time to set context—"We're going to do another task now"

4. Signal that the task instructions are beginning—"So what I want to do now is"

5. Structure the task stages—"I want you to discuss two things"

6. Manage behaviour—"In twos," "With a partner"

7. Set a time limit—"I'm going to give you 10 to 15 minutes"

8. Nominate—"What about this one, Juan?"

9. Check understanding—"So what have you got to do?"

10. Recap—"So that's what I want you to do"

11. Demonstrate/give example—"Marina, how would you describe to somebody what that is?"

12. Set students going on task—"Off you go"

INTERACTIONAL FEATURES OF PRETASK, TEACHER-FRONTED LESSON STAGES

During the workshop, the novice teachers also volunteered ideas about eliciting, for example, "deliver information asking questions at appropriate stages"; and about making modifications and adjustments to their normal speech, for example, "speak simply, uncluttered, less language rather than more," and "repeat instructions for lower levels." In their own lessons, they congratulated themselves for being concise, for paraphrasing, for directing questions at individuals by name, for eliciting rather than telling, and for praising their students. They mentioned the negative impact of using repetition when it was not needed and of striking the wrong tone in their relationship with students, for example, coming across to the students as "supercilious."

Nominating and checking are among the structural functions previously outlined, but names and checks are used differently for affective purposes. In the data, using names of people and places known to the learners and their teacher served to draw attention to shared experience, for example, "you went to Cambridge." Quick one-word checks such as "yeah," were an expedient to simulate interaction, for example, "just for 3 minutes, yeah?" Both of these strategies were helpful when setting up tasks, because they allowed teachers to hold onto their turn without having to relinquish it to a student, and thus to maintain momentum and focus for instruction giving.

Self-disclosure was another affective feature in the data, as teachers revealed aspects of their character or talked about their family life in personal anecdotes. This feature was often used to exemplify task requirements—"So, for example, something I'd like to buy, I'd like to buy a plane ticket to Australia to see my auntie." It also engendered community spirit in the class—"You all know me, I'm George, right? I want you to write me a letter, to me, Dear George, cos [because] we're all friends."

A final strategy identified as helpful for rapport was the use of the inclusive pronoun *we*. For example, "Remember when we were doing advice, those of us who were here?" Use of this pronoun allowed the teacher to project a view of teacher and students as a single entity, working together to achieve learning goals. "Everyone," "everybody," "no one," "nobody," "anyone," "anybody," "someone," "somebody," and occasionally "people" performed the same empathetic function as "we." For example, "OK. Good morning everybody. We'll start . . . anybody tell me what Nelson Mandela was famous for?"

The full taxonomy of interactional, rapport-enhancing rules that were drawn up during the workshop discussion are as follows:

- Use speech rate, pausing, and repetition (judiciously)—"Find page 52, Module 5 page 52."

- Elicit, rather than tell—"OK then, the first one. So what's this called in the middle?"

- Use quick checks, by single words or tag questions—"Don't we?" "Yes?"

- Use praise, by single words or longer comments—"Excellent," "Gosh, that's a new one!"

- Use names to personalise—"If you want to know about London you'll have to ask Edi."

- Use self-disclosure—"I'd like a ticket to Australia to see my auntie."

- Use inclusive *we* pronoun—"Hello, everyone." "Remember when we were doing advice?"

SUMMARY OF RESEARCH FINDINGS

In investigating preliminary issues of staging and interaction relevant to the use of tasks, I found that lessons in my data were staged in teacher-fronted and teacher-independent segments, with an attendant balance of teacher-student and student-student interaction patterns. In the setting up of the tasks, 12 rules were identified from the data relevant to a teacher's managerial role of structuring. In exploring features relevant to managing learning in pretask stages, I found that teachers made use of lexical phrases, with macro and micro discourse markers employed in predictable sequences, associated with lesson stage, preplanning, and task complexity. From the data, I identified the previous seven interactional rules as being relevant to a teacher's affective role of rapport-enhancing. In exploring issues around interactional features of pretask stages, I found that teachers personalised lesson content by nominating their learners or by referring to their involvement in shared experience. The teachers acknowledged or praised learner contributions, used self-disclosure, eliciting, checking, and the inclusive pronoun *we*. They also reported fostering interaction via adjustments in speech rate, pausing, and repetition.

Reflection

As a result of engaging in this study, I have begun to reflect more closely than previously on the functions of teacher-generated language in language classes taught through the target language. Moreover, in using entire lessons for my research, I have come to an appreciation of the richness and variety of teacher-generated language that serves as implicit instructive input to learners. I have identified in my data three broad categories of functions for teacher-generated language in task-based language lessons, as follows:

1. *Teaching function*—Help students construct, extend, or activate knowledge and understanding of language.

2. *Structuring function*—Structure and manage procedures conducive to language learning.

3. *Rapport-enhancing function*—Create and maintain positive affect through rapport.

From the evidence of my study, teacher-generated language in pretask stages emphasised structuring and rapport-enhancing. These are the two functions that I have described in this chapter and exemplified using my data. As a result of the research reported here, I have experimented with my discoveries in my teacher education activities. Using extracts from my data to show how teachers typically combine structuring and rapport-enhancing functions from the taxonomies, I have encouraged my novice teachers to notice how they use the target language in setting up tasks and to document what they find. This type of activity seems to help them analyse their own use of language more closely, as the following journal extract from a novice teacher shows:

Listening closely to this lesson reveals just how often I use the phrase "if you could . . ." as a task starter (about 12 times). At first I found this sounded quite polite, but after a while it did sound very repetitive and not really very authoritative at all, unlike the instruction I had previously observed being given. The one time I stepped away from this groove and used "I'd like you to . . ." I found that I immediately sounded far more "teacher-like" and in control. I realise now that although trying to be friendly to a class is all well and good (I believe this is what I was doing when using "if you could . . ."), it is far better to assume the teacher role and really lead a class in a task starter. It was also interesting to note that when I did use this alternative phrase, my instructions that followed were far more precise and succinct than any of the others in the lesson. ("I'd like you to discuss what you feel children should and shouldn't do, so thinking about the article and what John Roseman thinks, talk about what you think now." Perhaps not first-class, but a good improvement on a lot of the other waffle I had so far achieved!)

In follow-up work on the data from this study, I have found it fascinating to see how teachers can express individuality in the way they combine these two broad functions of structuring and rapport enhancing: One teacher may keep the two functions separate and associate them with specific lesson stages, and another teacher might integrate them more evenly across all lesson stages.

I hope my readers will be inspired to investigate their own use of classroom language and to explore the relative importance of it for teaching, structuring, and rapport enhancing in their own contexts.

Linda Taylor teaches at Nottingham Trent University in England.

CHAPTER 11

Do I Talk Too Much?
Exploring Dominant and Passive
Participation Dynamics (*Czech Republic*)

Jennifer E. Thomas

Issue

The impetus for my teacher research was a question that arose from my day-to-day experience in the classroom—why do some learners seem to talk all the time and yet others almost never share orally with the group? My attitude toward investigating that issue set the tone for the learners and opened the door for new insights to emerge. Inquisitiveness, enthusiasm, creativity, and a willingness to look beyond preconceived notions were essential. Additionally, the learners had to be active participants in the research, increasing their self-awareness, rather than just being objects of study. Purposefully, yet with flexibility, I designed a research plan which involved manageable changes in our classroom and careful observation of the results to see if the learners and I could learn anything valuable for our future interaction. The results revolutionized our culture of learning.

The context for this particular research was a content-based class on U.S. history at a Czech public college-preparatory high school. Participation in this advanced course was based on special entrance exams. Although the group officially had 10 members, only 6 were asked to participate in the research, based on their attendance (those who attended 30% of the time or less were not included). Having self-selected to join the program, the learners were generally motivated to learn and use English. However, their age and the realities of other school and life pressures (and perhaps the lack of formal credit and grades for the course) seemed to complicate their commitment. Although the exact nature of the course is perhaps not typical of most European high schools, I believe the findings about learner and teacher participation and the exploration of self-assessment can provide important insights for many teachers working with high school learners.

Learners in the Czech Republic, as in many other European countries, are required to study at least two foreign languages. At the end of high school, they take a rigorous oral leaving examination, for which they must be prepared to speak in their chosen foreign language for at least 10 minutes on one of 25 topics. This emphasis on content mastery often leads learners to memorize vast amounts of information which may be boring, irrelevant, or even incomprehensible to them. When asked to teach a special content-based course on U.S. history, I wrestled with how to make the content interesting and connect it with learners' lived experiences while also facilitating maximum English language development.

My primary goals for the U.S. history class were for learners to build communicative competence while gaining basic content knowledge through discussing and relating historical topics to their own history and life experiences. To my surprise and delight, the research we engaged in served to deepen our collective commitment to the learning task at hand. Our study communicated to the learners that what we were doing together mattered; in fact, it mattered so much that it was worth our time to intentionally explore it together and see how we could make it as valuable as possible.

Our research began during the second term of the year, which allowed me to reflect on the first term to identify a focus of inquiry. One primary issue rose to the surface: the tendency for the participation dynamic to be focused around me, as the teacher, or two or three dominant learners who spoke the majority of the time, offered opinions readily, asked and answered questions, and challenged others' viewpoints, sometimes quite aggressively. Although I valued these contributions and found myself feeling drawn to these learners, I wondered what was going on in the minds of the quieter learners and whether they were learning anything. I also began to wonder how the quieter ones felt about the more aggressive speakers—did they resent them, feel intimidated by them, respect or enjoy their contributions, or perhaps not care one way or another?

Background Literature

Rather than viewing learner and teacher participation as two separate issues, I came to see them as two sides of the same coin. Thus, in order to ground the research in relevant theory, I searched for material related to participation dynamics, especially dominant versus passive learners as well as the teacher's participation role. I approached the professional literature with a few specific questions: Is it helpful to encourage dominant learners to back off a bit or quieter ones to venture out and risk speaking more? Should I actively encourage this or simply allow them to decide on their own how to participate? And finally, how does the teacher's style and degree of participation influence learner participation?

Some theorists, such as Krashen and Terrell (1983), urge teachers to allow learners to speak when and how they feel comfortable. Along these lines, Cardoza (1994) found that dominant learners in her classroom would "create opportunities for themselves by speaking out rather than waiting to be called on" (p. 25), and the passive learners tended to speak more in structured scenarios, such as drills or being called on by the teacher. Although Cardoza's passive learners never transformed into aggressive speakers—even during lively class discussions about topics which all of the learners seemed interested in—she found that they were able and willing to write extensively in response to those discussions. Additionally, colleagues of these quieter learners reported that they used English competently outside of class. In the end, Cardoza concluded that forcing quieter learners to speak during class time was unnecessary.

However, in classes where communicative competence and speaking practice are key goals, teachers may want to design activities to encourage maximum verbal participation from all group members. Doughty and Pica (1986) found that information gap activities—in which each learner has information the others need to complete the task—facilitated more dynamic interaction between learners (especially interaction modifications such as clarification requests, confirmation, and comprehension checks) than group decision-making activities.

Doughty and Pica (1986) also compared teacher-centered versus learner-centered groups and found that, although there was more total interaction in the teacher-fronted group (largely because the teachers generated so much input), interaction modification was higher in the learner-to-learner groups. They speculated that perhaps learners were too intimidated to ask questions of the teacher or were afraid of showing a lack of understanding. Overall, their study found that learner-centered tasks with required information sharing among group members were most successful in promoting oral participation.

Building on the work of Doughty and Pica (1986), Alvarado (1992) added each learner's unique discourse style as a major factor in participation patterns. Her study found that differences in task types and teacher roles in the discussion were not enough to explain variations in learner participation. By pairing active and inactive learners in various groupings and on various tasks in both their first and second languages, Alvarado found that "speakers maintained similar patterns of participation regardless of the discourse style of their partners, the task type, or the language" (p. 591).

Sommers (1993) contributed to the discussion of learner participation dynamics by focusing on common problems in small-group interaction: lower proficiency learners offering redundant comments, fear of peer-response group work, dominant group members who interrupt others, and talented learners who overwhelm their partners because of the large gap in their skill levels. Convinced that the teacher has an important role to play in managing power dynamics in the classroom, Sommers found three possible options: (1) imposing rules and a structure to include all learners in peer interaction, (2) making the power issues explicit, or (3) allowing the groups to work through these issues without direct intervention.

In summary, the literature on participation dynamics suggests several key factors to consider in researching this topic: activity type (genuine communicative gaps seem to produce greater participation), learner participation and learning styles (which do not change easily), and the importance of the teacher's role (activity selection, increasing learner self-awareness, and promoting equitable distribution of classroom power).

Considering these findings about participation, I decided to explore the tool of authentic assessment, especially self-assessment, hoping it could help sensitize the learners and me to our styles, patterns, and degrees of participation. O'Malley and Valdez Pierce (1996) and Huerta-Macias (1995) highlighted alternative assessment for its emphasis not only on learning and achievement, but also on motivation and attitudes of the learners. McNamara and Deane (1995) argued for self-assessment, saying it can help students "identify their strengths and weaknesses in English" and "document their progress" (p. 17). Brown and Hudson (1998) further found that "the students' involvement and their greater autonomy can substantially increase their motivation to learn the language in question" (p. 666). Given the nontraditional nature of the history course and the fact that formal grades and traditional assessment are discouraged by the administration, self-assessment, with its emphasis on empowering and making learners more aware of their styles and degrees of participation and their progress toward their learning goals, seemed like a logical method to test out in the action research process.

With the problem coming more clearly into focus, I settled upon a research question to guide my inquiry: What happens in an English language classroom when the learners and the teacher reflect intentionally on their types and degrees of participation?

Procedures

CYCLE 1: SELF-REFLECTION ON PARTICIPATION

In order to encourage the learners to actively consider their degrees and styles of participation, I developed a brief questionnaire (see Appendix A), which they filled out at the end of three lessons, rating themselves on different types of participation and elaborating with comments. This self-assessment form covered several categories: listening to others, asking for information or clarification from the teacher and fellow learners, giving information in the form of facts or opinions, agreeing, and disagreeing. It also included a space for learners to detail their involvement in other forms of participation. To triangulate the data from learners' self-assessments, I invited a series of two outside observers to watch the first three research sessions, focusing on the learners' observable participation behaviors and filling out the same form about each learner. I also completed this form about each learner during or sometimes immediately after the lesson, thus providing three lenses through which to evaluate each learner's external and internal participation.

Alongside the learners' self-assessment, I kept a teacher journal, noting my participation and how it seemed to affect them. Based on the initial data collected, I made some methodological changes to the lessons, beginning in Cycle 1 and continuing throughout the term. My primary goal was to make the sessions more learner centered and facilitate increased learner talk time, which I attempted in two ways. First, I organized the seating in a circular pattern around a bank of desks, placing myself outside the circle, often seated in a chair several feet away from the learners. In so doing, I hoped to send a strong visual cue to support my assertion that the goal of the class was for them to build their content knowledge and communicative competence through talking with one another around historical topics. Second, shifting away from teacher-led discussion, I minimized my up-front presentation time and utilized written materials, discussion guides, pictures (such as political cartoons), jigsaw readings, and other handouts around which the learners could converse.

CYCLE 2: CONCRETE REPRESENTATIONS OF PARTICIPATION

The purpose of the self-assessment form was not just to gather information about the learners' thoughts and behavior, but also to help the learners become more conscious of them. To raise that consciousness to an even higher level, I introduced a system of participation cards for oral participation, which we used in three consecutive class periods. Each learner received seven cards (a different color for each person). Any comment or question during the discussion was accompanied by the participant putting one of his or her cards into a pile in the middle of the table. The goal for these cards was mainly to challenge those on the two extremes of the oral participation spectrum to notice and reflect on their behavior.

Two forms of record-keeping accompanied Cycle 2: (1) teacher observation notes; and (2) a more comprehensive self-assessment questionnaire (see Appendix B), which evaluated the learners' preferences related to type and degree of participation, including behaviors such as taking notes, writing ideas and journaling, discussing in pairs or small groups, and thinking about ideas on their own.

Between the second and third cycles, I used the information gathered about the learners (through their self-assessments, participation questionnaires, and my own and the observers' observations) to develop a one-page participation profile for each learner. I then asked the learners to modify their own profiles until they felt comfortable with the representation of their participation.

CYCLE 3: GOAL SETTING FOR PARTICIPATION

Based on their participation profiles, learners set participation goals for the remainder of the term, with an emphasis on stretching themselves in new ways and reflecting on how that participation related to their own and others' learning.

During this cycle, the learners checked in after each lesson with very brief surveys (see Appendix C) to reflect on their progress, whether the goal needed to be modified, and any results they saw in themselves or other learners as a result of their changes in behavior. At the end of the term, a final set of questions (see Appendix C) helped them elaborate on what they had learned through reflecting on their participation during the term.

During the several weeks in which we worked through Cycle 3, a few significant problems arose. Attendance, which had been much steadier during the second cycle, again became sporadic. Several learners missed the initial goal-setting session, requiring me to brief them one-on-one in later lessons and decreasing the amount of feedback I received from them about their progress toward their goals. Additionally, some learners resisted creating goals or chose goals that I found counter to the type of participation I was hoping to encourage (e.g., "I will not ask so many questions"). Feeling the pressure not to take too much time away from our limited sessions (we met only once a week for 45 minutes), I interacted only briefly with learners about these issues, ultimately making the goal-setting process weaker than it might have been had we devoted more time to it. However, looking at the results of the study, I found that the learners still considered the exercise valuable.

Results

Before detailing the results of the study, it is important to introduce the six participators.[1] Coincidentally, the group broke into three pairs categorized by typical degrees of participation: Ruben and Marketa (dominant participators), Georgia and Jennifer (midrange participators), and Kate and Michelle (passive participators).

CYCLE 1: SELF-REFLECTION ON PARTICIPATION

The most obvious result of Cycle 1 was a dramatic increase in oral participation by some of the learners, particularly the midrange participators, Georgia and Jennifer. The most passive learners, Kate and Michelle, also spoke more than they had in the past, which was virtually not at all. Despite the evidence in their self-assessments that they were grappling with changing their behavior, Ruben and Marketa were still the most dominant speakers in the group. Although Ruben sometimes tried to ask the quieter learners their opinions, he did not leave very much wait time before moving on to another idea, and they often did not respond. Another interesting result was that Marketa, who had always been one of the most active speakers, gradually participated less and less during the first two cycles. This was a surprising and disappointing result, although it changed favorably later in the term.

Some significant differences arose between the learners' participation self-assessments and the assessments by outside observers and me. I particularly noted some key variations between learners' and my own concepts of what participation meant. For example, on several occasions the more passive learners indicated that they were actively participating in their minds, by agreeing or disagreeing with classmates' ideas. Because this mental activity was unobservable, neither the outside observers nor I noted it as participation. Other significant discrepancies in the assessments occurred when it was difficult to observe the behavior, such as listening or asking other learners for information—which often occurred during pair work when the observers' attention was divided. In general, I assumed that the learners were listening to each other if they replied to others' comments or exhibited body language such as eye contact, leaning forward, or laughing. However, some learners who appeared to be listening, according to this standard, reported that they were not always doing so (as seen in Ruben's comment: "Sometimes I just don't pay attention to others"). Other learners, like Kate and Michelle, were often very difficult to read, exhibiting almost no body language, yet reporting that they were listening actively and with interest.

The category of "giving information" revealed an interesting insight, namely that although I conceived of this category as including times when the learners presented information they had just read in class (e.g., in jigsaw activities), the learners believed they were only giving information when they shared knowledge they had about the topic outside of anything we had studied together.

Preconceived notions about the learners—whether their own, the observers', or mine—were also difficult to avoid and may have affected the assessments. This was especially true when behavior seemed to differ significantly from learners' past patterns, as when Marketa self-consciously decreased her oral participation during the first two research cycles because she feared that others resented her frequent questions and comments.

Turning to the results of my self-reflection, examining my teacher journal quickly made me aware of how easily I could fall into dominating patterns of participation. After the first session, I wrote the following:

> *I* instigated almost all of the questions and many of the clarifications; *I* chose the texts and assigned them to the learners (rather than allowing them to choose which one they wanted to read); *I* encouraged them to describe things more deeply or expand on their answers; *I* asked on a few occasions if the other learner agreed.

Additionally, I noticed in the first session that the participation dynamic seemed to be teacher-to-learner and learner-to-teacher, but not learner-to-learner. I observed the following:

> As they speak, they seem to be directing their speech toward me and not toward each other. Could this be related to where they're sitting? (Next to each other, facing me.) What would happen if I moved myself out of the circle?

I then rearranged the physical layout into a circle and sat outside it, encouraging students to speak about discussion questions, political cartoons, and other written materials. This arrangement produced some dramatic results in participation dynamics. Some learners initially expressed feeling uncomfortable with being observed by me while they talked (such as Jennifer who commented that she "felt like an animal in a zoo"), but most said they found it easier to share their thoughts and noticed increased oral participation from other learners.

CYCLE 2: CONCRETE REPRESENTATIONS OF PARTICIPATION

Throughout the three sessions in which we used participation cards, all of the learners exhibited an increase in oral participation, using more and more cards in each session. The only exception was Jennifer, the only learner who used all seven cards in all three lessons (and clearly wished for more). Their evaluations of Cycle 2 shed some light on the benefits and drawbacks of using these cards (see Table 1). Whether or not there was a connection, it is interesting to note that the learners who were typically midrange participators both felt very positive about the cards (to their own surprise), and the two typically dominant participators had more mixed feelings.

Table 1. Learner Evaluations of Participation Card System

Learner	Typical Degree of Participation	Number of Cards Used in Sessions	Comments
Overall Positive Reactions			
Jennifer	Midrange	7, 7, 7	"Actually, I liked those cards, because I can think about what I'm doing here and what I'm doing bad or right."
Georgia	Midrange	5, 6, 6	"I was little bit surprised, but I like [the participation cards]. It's clever idea. Before this we didn't know exactly how active we are. Seven cards are for some topic enough, but for some other it is too few for me. But I never used all of my cards."
Kate	Passive	3, 5, 6	"At first I thought it's too much, but it's not true. When you really know many thing about the theme you need more. But as you know, for me it was enough."
Ambivalent or Negative Reactions			
Ruben	Dominant	6, 7, 7	"At first I thought it isn't the right way to go, it would just spoil the discussion. Definitely for me it was too few. After lesson it wasn't so bad though. Seven are quite enough and it regulates how much will all people say in one hour."
Marketa	Dominant	3, 6, 7	"I was a little bit confused and surprised because I have never done this before [used participation cards]. I like speaking in English as much as I can so it is for me something difficult not to speak when I have not enough papers. But anyway, it's good. But on the other hand, I think it doesn't make the less speaking pupils to participate. Maybe only a little. For me is better to have a discussion without papers on some theme."
Michelle	Passive	3, absent, absent	"I like this idea but seven cards are too much for me. Maybe it is a little bit press, but it more encourage us to discuss together."

The learners' comments in Table 1 point out some of the benefits I hoped would result from using the participation cards. In particular, the learners seemed to become more aware of how much they were speaking, to feel encouraged to take risks in communicating (being "pressed" a bit, as Michelle said), and to see others become more involved (both dominant participators had expressed their desire for this, although only Ruben felt it had happened to a significant degree). Table 1 also highlights some of the drawbacks of using the cards, including the frustration that ensues from not having enough cards to say what one wants and the reality that the cards do not force the "less speaking pupils," as Marketa called them, to increase their participation.

CYCLE 3: GOAL SETTING ABOUT PARTICIPATION

The third cycle was by far the most difficult for the learners; however, the results were encouraging. Most of them were initially resistant to setting goals, but by the end the majority expressed various ways in which the process had been valuable to them. Their goals (see Table 2) begin to tell the story of their journeys.

Marketa's goals and reflections on her progress show a clear fear of others' perceptions about her participation, including her teacher's perception. After I reassured her on several occasions that her comments and questions were valued, she became enthusiastic about the changes in the lessons and reported enjoying the learner-centered discussions very much: "I was so happy I could listen to opinions of my schoolmates—they were great and I was able to put all their ideas and to mix it with my own."

Ruben initially did not want to make any changes to his way of participating, feeling that the problem lay with the more passive learners rather than with him. Over time, however, he came to see that he could play a role in helping them open up. He commented at the end, "I changed little bit direction of my effort, firstly I tried just to be more quiet, but afterwards I recognized it's not enough so I wanted to cooperate with others. That was right and useful change." Georgia's reflections show the clearest progression from skeptic to believer in the goal-

Table 2. Learner Goals

Learner	Goals Expressed
Marketa	"Not to speak too much and disturb my schoolmates. Not to ask too many questions. Try to think more about any historical topic. Try to ask others."
Ruben	"Work more with others."
Georgia	"Try to share my opinion at least one time in every lesson, even if I'm a little bit uncomfortable." (later changed to 2 or 3 times per lesson)
Jennifer	"Try not to be shy about speaking English."
Kate	"Try to speak more—3? times in each lesson?"
Michelle	"To be more open to current events and more often watching TV news and read political news in newspapers."

setting process. She remarked, "I see that this system—to make some goal—is effective. I really speak more and more and I don't have bigger problems with it now."

Jennifer's goal was interesting because she deliberately set an internal goal. She struggled with whether or not to change it, but decided that her shyness about speaking was really something she wanted to focus her attention on. Ultimately, she progressed, noting, "I felt excited and a bit scared (but the fear was smaller than before)." Kate had a straightforward and measurable goal and felt positive about her progress: "Now it's easier to participate than at the beginning of the year."

Michelle's goal was the most challenging for me to understand. She explained that she wanted to increase her knowledge of current events to strengthen her ability to participate in class discussions. However, she reported that she was too busy to meet her goal and yet did not feel it was necessary to change it. Her comments also highlighted a common assertion for many learners—that oral participation hinged on their comfort level with the topic being discussed.

With respect to my goal of reducing my dominant role in the participation dynamic, I felt very good overall about the results, but sometimes had mixed feelings. This was particularly true at points when I felt passionately about the topic of discussion (e.g., feminism, terrorism) and wanted to push the learners to consider the issues from a different angle. At times some learners would look at me as though appealing for me to join them—often to counter a strong opinion expressed by a dominant learner. I usually refrained from doing so and was pleased to see others step in to articulate opposing viewpoints. In general, it was a learning process for all of us. The learners needed time to learn how to be more autonomous, and I needed practice as well!

Reflection

What did I learn from taking on the dual role of teacher and researcher in a European secondary school classroom? Many readers of this chapter may, like me, teach high school learners. We can easily succumb to complaining about their laziness, the volume of material we are expected to help them master, and the necessity to teach to a test. These frustrations can lead to teacher-centered classrooms where angry teachers struggle fruitlessly with bored, bitter learners, or settle for a running dialogue with a few rare enthusiastic ones while their peers doodle and daydream the hours away. Instead of placing a strict curriculum or a high-stakes exam at the center of the educational environment, we as teachers can choose to focus learning around empowering learners through self-reflection, risk taking, and goal setting. If we take this approach, perhaps we can break down some of the harmful participation dynamics so typical in traditional

European classrooms and move toward a new culture of learning. Keeping that broad lesson in mind, I turn now to some of the specific insights gained from this particular experience with teacher research.

INSIGHTS FROM PASSIVE PARTICIPATORS

From reading the comments and observing the behavior of the more passive learners, I discovered three valuable things:

1. **They are content with listening and feel that they learn from it.** If I am to take their word at face value, learners such as Kate and Michelle appreciate discussion even though they do not actively contribute to it. Because real-life communication does not offer or require equal participation from all interlocutors, perhaps it is reasonable to allow learners to interact as they feel most comfortable.

2. **They may feel intimidated by dominant learners and by open-ended, debate-style discussions.** In their study of learner participation in decision-making activities, Doughty and Pica (1986) observed that open-ended discussions did not encourage much communication from passive learners. They noted that these activities, "while communicative in emphasis, were nevertheless not required information exchange tasks" (p. 307). Doughty and Pica's findings were consistent with those of my study in that passive learners tended to remain quiet during unstructured large-group discussions and debates.

3. **For the most part, they will remain consistent with their discourse style, but they can be encouraged to stretch themselves.** Although open-ended discussions may not be the most effective way to get passive learners to speak, information gap activities (such as the jigsaw readings we did at certain points) have great potential because these learners have information that is needed by their peers. Other activities, such as writing or silent reflection, can also be helpful with learners whose learning style is not speaking-oriented but who enjoy other ways of participating. Cardoza (1994) found that "the important thing is to provide a stimulus for meaningful interaction, then follow up with opportunities for each learner to use an individual learning style in responding" (p. 27). This is one area where I could have been more effective with the passive participators, and I will try to use this strategy more in the future.

INSIGHTS FROM DOMINANT PARTICIPATORS

The dominant participators, largely due to the ease with which they could articulate their reflections and preferences, taught me three lessons as well:

1. **They viewed the history class as an opportunity to practice speaking—first and foremost.** The primacy of this goal led them to struggle with self-consciousness or even anger about the gap between their oral participation and that of the quieter learners. Even Jennifer, who vacillated between the two groups but was a dominant force when the topic was of personal interest to her, wrote the following: "Sometimes I think [the other learners] don't like me to speak." But these dominant ones *can* learn to channel their speaking abilities to encourage others into communicating. As Ruben testified, "I think more about what's going on in other people's minds—they are actually trying to improve their work, so let's cooperate more!"

2. **They may disengage if they do not feel they are getting what they want from the lessons.** Although this may not be true for all, the dominant learners in my group were not as enthusiastic about participating through writing or reading. According to Ruben, at many times it was frustrating to listen to the others, and he simply chose not to at times. The key was talking with these dominant learners about their frustrations, allowing them to express their feelings, and encouraging them to find positive outlets for their communicative energy.

3. **They too will tend to follow their discourse style, but their style can benefit all.** These oral processors enjoy dialogue and debate. They are genuinely good at these activities and often have valuable things to contribute to the discussion, which other learners indicate they appreciate and learn from. As Sommers (1993) pointed out, when teachers impose rules of participation on all learners, "those gifted and articulate learners who would otherwise speak often and well are . . . muted for the presumed good of the whole peer response group" (p. 9). When they are encouraged to reach out to others, their gifts can draw their peers in.

INSIGHTS ABOUT TEACHER PARTICIPATION

By reviewing my own approach and interactions I learned the following:

- **I cannot avoid playing a role in the participation dynamic; however, I can choose what my role will be.** The teacher-dominated dynamic I noted in my journal was at odds with my overall goal of having learners engage with one another in authentic discussions. My approach ultimately became one of making participation and classroom power dynamics explicit—encouraging the learners to become aware of and talk with each other about their participation while taking risks and trying new ways of interacting with one another.

- **It is risky to allow learners more autonomy, but the risk is worthwhile.** Throughout the process I struggled with misgivings. My success at facilitating several learner-centered lessons during the term was satisfying but also left me wondering: Did the learners really learn more this way? Did any of them resent me for stepping back? One advantage was allowing (perhaps forcing) them to negotiate for meaning with one another. Overall, though, I was able to see significant growth in the learners and watch a new culture of learning gradually develop among us. The payoff was worth the risks.

Marketa's words poignantly summarized the heart of this inquiry. *Do I talk too much? Or perhaps too little?*

> I have to say that I'm not the kind of pupil who goes home and to the table to study. But English is something different. I love this language and for me it is great. . . . I'm so talkative that I try to speak as much as I can. I have to hope that others will understand me.

No one in this study, including me, felt completely comfortable with his or her ways of participating. The dominant learners questioned others' reactions to them and the passive learners often found themselves waiting for the right topic which would provide a safe opportunity to risk speaking out. However, I have also found it important to honor the learner's right to choose not to participate orally in a particular discussion. This reality requires me as the teacher to walk a fine line. My role lies in designing learning opportunities that entice the learners to choose to engage, or at least keep them open-minded long enough to consider the opportunity fully.

This study has been a foundation which I plan to build upon with this group (and other groups) in the future. Using discussion guides, information gap activities, and other written materials has been helpful. I hope to augment these tools with activities that engage different learning styles—especially more writing activities (perhaps through journaling or interacting through a class blog on the Internet). Sharing this research experience together has built trust and openness among the group, which I hope to capitalize upon as we continue to reflect on how our ways of participating can enhance our learning experiences together.

Jennifer E. Thomas teaches at Gymnazium Pripotocni
secondary school in Prague, Czech Republic.

Note

1. Pseudonyms have been substituted for the real names of the participants.

Appendix A: Self-Assessment of Participation Questionnaire (Cycle 1)

Name: _____ Date: _____

How often did you do the following things in the lesson today?

Please check (✓) the box that best describes your response and add comments.

Task	Not at All	Rarely	Sometimes	Often	Comments
I listened to others while they were speaking.					
I asked for information from the teacher.					
I asked for information from other students.					
I gave information.					
I gave an opinion.					
I agreed or disagreed.					
I asked for clarification of something I didn't understand.					
Other participation: Taking notes Reading a text Thinking about the text . . .					

Appendix B: Participation Behavior Questionnaire (Cycle 2)

Name: _____ Date: _____

Please circle the number that best describes your own attitude or behavior.

	Very little	Some-what	Very much
1. I enjoy participating in whole class discussions.	1	2	3
2. I enjoy participating in pair discussions.	1	2	3
3. I prefer thinking about a topic rather than speaking about it.	1	2	3
4. I prefer to write my ideas rather than speak them.	1	2	3
5. In a group, I need time before I am ready to speak.	1	2	3
6. I like to speak immediately when a question is asked.	1	2	3
7. I enjoy sharing my opinion.	1	2	3
8. I feel uncomfortable sharing my opinion.	1	2	3
9. Sharing my opinion is easier in pairs than in groups.	1	2	3
10. I prefer talking to other students rather than to the teacher.	1	2	3
11. I prefer talking to the teacher rather than to other students.	1	2	3
12. One way I like to participate is by taking notes.	1	2	3
13. I learn better when I am speaking or discussing.	1	2	3
14. I learn better when I am writing.	1	2	3
15. I learn better when I am quietly reflecting on my own.	1	2	3
16. I learn better when I am reading.	1	2	3
17. I learn better when I am listening to others speak.	1	2	3
18. I feel frustrated when others dominate discussions.	1	2	3
19. I feel frustrated when others are quiet in discussions.	1	2	3
20. Because I don't speak a lot, I feel that I am not participating as much as other students.	1	2	3

Please give a detailed and specific answer to these questions. The more information you can give, the more helpful your answer will be.

1. How did you feel when you first heard that we would be using "participation cards" in the last lesson? Did you at first think that 7 cards would be too many or too few for you? Did your opinion change by the end of the lesson?

2. What is your own learning style? What kinds of participation help you to understand, process, and remember the information best?

3. Do you think that the other students respect, understand, and/or appreciate your personal ways of participating? Do you think they feel you participate too much or too little? What is your response to what they might think about your participation?

Appendix C: Goal Questionnaire (Cycle 3)

Name: _____

Date: _____

My participation goal for the rest of the year:

1. Do you see any need to make a change to your goal (to make it more manageable, easier to measure, or more challenging)?

2. Did you try to meet your goal today? Why or why not?

3. How did you feel as you were trying (frustrated, scared, excited, challenged, interested, bored)? Why?

4. Did you notice any impact on yourself or on others because of the changes you made?

Year-End Questions

1. What did you learn from reflecting on your own participation this term?

2. How do you feel now about your goal now at the end of the term?

3. Do you think you will do anything differently in the future because of what you've learned through this experience?

CHAPTER 12

Multiple Intelligences Come to the University: A Case Study (*Turkey*)

Eda Üstünel

Issue

In this chapter, I explore ways of adapting Multiple Intelligences Theory (MIT) to the needs of English language teacher trainees in Turkey. This is an original undertaking in the sense that although MIT has been used in educational contexts in general (Armstrong, 1994; Campbell, 1997; Lazear, 1991; Marzano et al., 1988; Nicholson-Nelson, 1998, Teele, 2000) and in the second and foreign language classroom in particular (Christison, 1997, 1998, 1999, 2001; Reid, 1997; Smagorinsky, 1995), I am not aware of cases in which it has been applied to the teaching of content courses for language teacher trainees. This chapter outlines my attempts to do this in my context.

In January 2005 I was assigned for the first time to teach a linguistics module to second-year preservice Turkish teachers of English. I had studied linguistics in both my undergraduate and postgraduate studies but never actually taught it. This would also be the first time those particular trainees had studied linguistics, and in informal conversations before I began teaching they indicated that their feelings about the subject were not positive. They strongly believed that linguistics is a difficult module based on theoretical input and with no scope for fun in the classroom.

I spent considerable time thinking about which teaching method or theory I should use to make the module content clear and to ensure the active participation of the trainees in classroom activities. As a first step, I asked the trainees to complete the VARK learning style questionnaire (Fleming, 2006) to find out which types of learners I would be working with. Educators can find many questionnaires of this kind in the literature (e.g., Smith & Kolb, 1986; Tarone & Yule, 1989). In this case, I chose the VARK questionnaire for the following reasons:

- It was one of the more recently published instruments.

- The questions were easy to follow with simple sentence structure and familiar vocabulary items.

- The questionnaire was readily available on the Internet, with ease of duplication.

- The results of the questionnaire were not calculated by counting the number of each choice, unlike most learning style questionnaires. Rather, the questionnaire itself provided a results chart through which a particular learner style could be matched with specific answers.

The results of the questionnaire indicated that I had a class of trainees with different learning styles. It was also clear, though, that a number of trainees were largely kinesthetic, which means that they would not enjoy sitting still and listening silently to teacher input. With the help of the VARK questionnaire results, I settled down to apply MIT in teaching the linguistics module in order to make the course appealing to students with different types of intelligences.

Background Literature

The theory of multiple intelligences was proposed by Gardner (1983) as a result of his work with brain-damaged patients in a Boston-area hospital (Hoerr, 1996b, p. 9). Gardner (1997) defined *intelligence* as the "capacity to solve problems or to fashion products that are valued in one or more cultural settings" (p. 120). His basic view was that human intelligence has multiple dimensions that must be acknowledged and developed in education (Richards & Rodgers, 2001). Teele (1996) used the analogy of a window to define MIT:

The theory of multiple intelligences provides different windows into the same room. We need to unleash the creative potential in all our schools to open as many windows as possible for every student to succeed. We must move forward together in a way that builds on our mutual strengths and respects our unique differences. (p. 75)

Gardner further proposed that his view of intelligence is culture-free and avoids the conceptual narrowness usually associated with traditional models of intelligence. Without doubt, those views encourage the application of MIT in education. Every year more schools are added to the growing list of MI schools, and hundreds of studies, articles, and books on MIT continue to appear. MIT represents a model that places student understanding at the forefront of educational reform. Today, Gardner's theory serves as one of the most effective curricular and instructional frameworks for classroom teachers to use in designing their teaching. His theory provides one approach that at least attempts to address the multiple ways of learning and understanding that students bring with them to the language classroom (Hoerr, 1996a, p. 36).

The eight native intelligences that Gardner proposed are described in Table 1 (Campbell, Campbell, & Dickinson, 1996; Mjagkij & Cantu, 1999).

Gardner's theory of intelligence thus goes well beyond the traditional focus on logical-mathematical and linguistic intelligence—quite often the sole focus of standardized tests and classroom instruction (Gardner & Hatch, 1989; Teele, 1996). In relation to this point, Campbell and Campbell (1999) concluded in their research in traditional classrooms that 70% of class time was occupied with teacher talk, and the remaining 30% was used for class activities, an arrangement which students find boring. In language classrooms too, most of the time is taken up with teacher talk. On the other hand, the teacher who embraces MIT consciously adopts teaching methods which will appeal to different intelligences. I do not mean that instruction should never be teacher centred. Such instruction, though, should not be the sole experience learners have—it is but one of many possibilities which teachers can utilise.

Table 1. Summary of Gardner's Eight Intelligences

Form of Intelligence	Central Components
Logical/Mathematical	Discern logical or numerical patterns; use deductive reasoning
Verbal/Linguistic	Use written and spoken language to express complex meaning
Visual/Spatial	Perceive the visual world accurately; create mental images
Musical/Rhythmic	Produce and appreciate forms of musical expressiveness
Body/Kinesthetic	Control body movements and handle items skilfully
Naturalist	Recognize patterns and distinctions in the natural world
Interpersonal	Understand others; discern verbal and nonverbal cues
Intrapersonal	Understand oneself; engage in self-reflection and metacognition

To sharpen the distinction between traditional and MI classrooms, Table 2 outlines MI instructional strategies designed for each form of intelligence (Chapman, 1993; Meyer, 1997; Weber, 1996). As Table 2 indicates, the most important implication of MIT for education is that it expands the teacher's repertoire of instructional strategies in such a way that these extend beyond the verbal/linguistic domain (which traditional education focuses on) and addresses a wider range of intelligences.

Armstrong (1994) argued that MIT is a framework which allows teachers to rethink school education. In particular, it allows teachers to reconsider the way they describe learners who fail to make progress. Traditionally, such learners are described as having learning difficulties. From an MIT perspective, it is teachers, rather, who have teaching difficulties. For example, teachers are often reluctant to adapt their teaching styles to different learning styles. Or teachers may adhere to a limited range of instructional activities. MIT provides teachers with a framework to reflect on these issues and to consider alternatives.

In fact, the concept of learning difficulty runs counter to the basic thinking behind MIT. Students who learn in ways which do not match the instruction provided by teachers should not be described as having learning problems. For example, sitting still in a classroom for a long time is against the nature of kinesthetic learners, and these learners are often unfairly labelled as hyperactive. Similarly, visual learners, who have some problems understanding abstract entities, are labelled as reading handicapped (Armstrong, 1987, 1988).

Another appealing element of the MI framework is that it allows teachers to teach in a manner that does not ask them to sacrifice verbal and analytical skills

Table 2. MI Instructional Strategies

Form of Intelligence	Teaching Activities
Logical/Mathematical	Problem solving, investigation, experimentation, questioning
Verbal/Linguistic	Discussion, narration, advanced organizers, writing activities
Visual/Spatial	Imagery, map analysis, observation activities, construction of dioramas or posters
Musical/Rhythmic	Simulations, song analysis, creative song writing, performances
Body/Kinesthetic	Simulations, modelling, role playing, analyzing manipulatives
Naturalist	Recognizing and classifying cultural and natural artifacts, data gathering in natural setting
Interpersonal	Cooperative learning, peer teaching, brainstorming, shared inquiry
Intrapersonal	Decision making, journal writing, self-discovery, independent learning projects

for what some might term more affective or nontraditional forms of intelligence (Knodt, 1997; Latham, 1997). Instead, it offers educators an instructional framework which can promote in students the deeper understanding Gardner (1993) defined as "a sufficient grasp of concepts, principles, or skills so that you can bring them to bear on new problems and situations" (p. 21). The flexibility of MIT was important in my context, a university setting which generally promoted verbal and analytical skills.

Procedures

In this study, I aimed to answer the following research question: Is MIT compatible with teaching linguistics on a university degree programme? The research procedures I adopted related primarily to the design and implementation of the linguistics course I taught. My data thus consisted of the course materials I developed, the work the trainees produced, and my observations of how the materials worked in practice. I also collected some data from my trainees about their views of the course. The bulk of my effort, though, went into the design and delivery of the course.

The study participants were second-year undergraduates in a four-year initial teacher training programme. The trainees were 20 to 21 years of age, and they were already proficient in English but had no prior experience studying linguistics.

The Introduction to Linguistics I course consists of 3 class hours per week throughout one academic term (15 weeks). Richards and Rodgers (2001) noted that "there is no syllabus as such, either prescribed or recommended, in respect to MI-based language teaching" (p. 118). However, Lazear (1991) proposed a basic developmental sequence as an alternative to a syllabus design. The sequence has four stages, and the following description provides a sense of my overall course structure using those four stages:

1. **Awaken the intelligence.** At the start of the course I brought many different teaching materials to class, such as phonics-teaching CDs with human voices, morphology-related flashcards, and syntactical board games. My aim in using such materials was to make learners aware of the practical uses of abstract linguistic terms in their daily lives and to encourage them to see that linguistics was not necessarily a dry theoretical subject.

2. **Amplify the intelligence.** I asked trainees to bring objects (e.g., texts) to class and discuss in groups how they might use these as the basis of classroom teaching materials. These discussions focused on the three main areas of linguistics we were dealing with—phonetics and phonology, morphology, and syntax. The aim here was to start encouraging the trainees to

think of how they might handle such issues with their students when they became English language teachers.

3. **Teach with/for the intelligence.** I structured larger sections of lessons so as to reinforce and emphasise the classroom language that they could use in teaching the three main areas of linguistics. Trainees worked in groups, for example, to design a lesson plan about word-formation process by analysing some cartoons which I provided.

4. **Transfer of the intelligence.** This fourth stage is concerned with the application of intelligence to students' daily lives. I asked trainees to reflect on the content of the linguistics module and its operational procedures in their daily lives outside the classroom.

In structuring the course, I sought ways of building in this kind of repeated cycle to support trainees' understandings of the different topics we covered.

In addition to thinking about the overall structure of the course, I needed to develop specific materials for each session on the course. My aim was to address all eight intelligences (as shown in Table 1) in each week's session, but this was not always easy to achieve. I also found the information in Table 2 helpful as a means of identifying classroom activities for teaching linguistics which would relate to different forms of intelligence. Tables 3 and 4 summarise the teaching activities and teacher resources I used in relation to the different forms of intelligence.

To illustrate the approach I adopted, I describe here the design of the first session on the course in detail. In the first week of the term, after giving the module outline to the class, I started the course by defining *linguistics*. Before the class, I gathered some definitions from various English and Turkish books and articles. I printed them on a transparency and projected these on the board. I then asked the students to work in groups to classify the definitions in terms of their themes (e.g., cultural aspects of a language, information about language systems, information on the origin of a language). This activity appeals to various intelligences: logical/mathematical (problem solving and questioning), verbal/linguistic (discussion), naturalist (classify cultural and natural artifacts), interpersonal (brainstorming, cooperative learning, peer teaching), and intrapersonal (decision making, self-discovery).

Then I asked each group to choose one theme from those they identified and to analyse the lyrics of a song in the light of that theme. I played the song once before they started the activity and played it again as they carried out the activity. This activity appealed to musical/rhythmic intelligence in addition to the intelligences mentioned in the categorising activity. Later, I asked them to prepare a poster based on their thematic analysis of the song. I brought to class a tool kit which contained big cartoons, magazines with lots of pictures, scissors,

Table 3. MI-Based Linguistics Activities

Form of Intelligence	Teaching Activities	Course Content
Logical/ Mathematical	Categorise the course contents; find similarities and differences between linguistic terms	Definition of linguistics, major subfields of linguistics, the linguistic use of sound (phonology), suprasegmentals (intonation levels), word classes, syntax
Verbal/ Linguistic	Compose essays; critique written resources through an annotated bibliography; do student-group project work via storytelling and brainstorming; listen to cassettes, CDs, and videos	Definition of linguistics, the functions of language, the sounds of speech (phonetics), suprasegmentals (intonation levels)
Visual/Spatial	Draw charts, diagrams, and pictures; use mind maps and visualisation of linguistic processes	Definition of linguistics, major subfields of linguistics, the functions of language, the linguistic use of sound (phonology), word classes, morphology
Musical/ Rhythmic	Analyse song lyrics; design and publish PowerPoint presentations which incorporate music and visual elements	Definition of linguistics, the origins of language, the sounds of speech (phonetics), suprasegmentals (intonation levels), word classes, syntax
Body/ Kinesthetic	Do cooperative Web searches, role-playing activities, and classroom presentations	Definition of linguistics, major subfields of linguistics, the origins of language, the functions of language, the linguistic use of sound (phonology), morphology, syntax
Naturalist	Analyze world map and city maps for linguistic processes in proper names	The origins of language, the linguistic use of sound (phonology), word classes
Interpersonal	Work in groups and pairs; do peer teaching in the classroom and brainstorming in groups	Definition of linguistics, major subfields of linguistics, the functions of language, the sounds of speech (phonetics), suprasegmentals (intonation levels), syntax
Intrapersonal	Fill in a reflective questionnaire applied at the end of project work	The origins of language, the functions of language, the linguistic use of sound (phonology), word classes

Table 4. MI-Based Linguistics Resources

Form of Intelligence	Teaching Resources	Course Content
Logical/ Mathematical	Charts, diagrams, tables, statistical and population data	Major subfields of linguistics, the origins of language, the functions of language, the linguistic use of sound (phonology), morphology
Verbal/ Linguistic	Written projects, articles, books, personal narratives, historical documents, letters	The origins of language, the functions of language, the sounds of speech (phonetics), word classes, syntax
Visual/Spatial	Maps, diagrams, illustrations, historical documents	Definition of linguistics, major subfields of linguistics, the origins of language, the sounds of speech (phonetics), morphology, syntax
Musical/ Rhythmic	Lyrics or audio files of songs	Definition of linguistics, the functions of language, the sounds of speech (phonetics), suprasegmentals (intonation levels), word classes
Body/ Kinesthetic	Illustrations and descriptions of linguistic processes for role playing	Definition of linguistics, major subfields of linguistics, the sounds of speech (phonetics), suprasegmentals (intonation levels), morphology, syntax
Naturalist	Illustrations, paintings, maps, photographs of linguistics terms such as place names	The origins of language, the functions of language, the linguistic use of sound (phonology), word classes
Interpersonal	All of the above resources that might be used in cooperative MI activities	Definition of linguistics, major subfields of linguistics, the sounds of speech (phonetics), suprasegmentals (intonation levels), morphology
Intrapersonal	All of the above resources that might be used in reflective, individual MI activities	The origins of language, the functions of language, the linguistic use of sound (phonology), suprasegmentals (intonation levels), syntax

colourful pens, stickers, and glue, and advised the students that they could design their posters in any way they liked as long as it represented the analysis of the song. The poster activity appealed to visual/spatial intelligence (imagery and construction of posters). As a final group activity, I asked them to write an analogy for linguistics (e.g., "linguistics is the study of a language," "it is like making a jigsaw," "it is like baking a cake") and act it out or draw a picture about it on the board. The last activity appealed to body/kinesthetic intelligence (simulations, role playing, and modelling).

Table 3 outlines additional types of activities which teachers might incorporate into MI-based linguistics lessons. A wide repertoire of activities such as this is essential for the effective implementation of MIT, although it should be clear, as my experience has demonstrated, that developing the resources to implement such activities calls for a significant amount of effort. At the same time, MIT allows teachers to be flexible in the way that different activities are designed, interpreted, and used. My experience suggests that this flexibility is an additional strength of using MIT in teacher education.

Results

As I noted earlier, the primary forms of data resulting from this study were the materials and activities through which I implemented MIT on the linguistics module for trainee teachers. Tables 3 and 4 are in essence a summary of the key results here: They demonstrate how it was possible to apply MIT to foreign language teacher education. Primary and high school English language teachers have been using multiple intelligences lesson plans for some time. My work shows that English language teacher educators can adopt MIT in their work too. I believe this is an innovation that, if widely adopted, can enhance the quality of preservice language teacher education in Turkey.

Three benefits of the MIT teaching strategy highlighted by Gardner (1995) were evident from my experience. First, because not all students learn in the same way, English language teacher trainers are able to meet the needs of more trainees in their classes. Second, the trainees can realize that linguists, teachers, and students view linguistics from a variety of perspectives and that this awareness provides a stronger basis for the trainees' study of linguistics. Finally, the MI model allows students to demonstrate their understandings in a variety of ways, including posters, cartoons, storytelling, Internet (online) annotated bibliographies, student-generated PowerPoint presentations, and Internet links pages. These options were a completely new, but very welcome experience for my trainees, who were mostly accustomed to conventional forms of demonstrating understanding. My observations of the course, including an analysis of the work the trainees produced, supported the view that MIT can be usefully applied to content courses on language teacher education programmes.

Feedback from the trainees pointed towards similarly positive views. They completed evaluation forms at the end of the course, and some quotes from these reflect their opinions on the work we did together. The trainees agreed that the course content was easy to comprehend (contrary to their concerns prior to the course). In explaining this, one trainee wrote, "We learn without noticing that we are learning." Another trainee said that comprehension was assisted by opportunities to link theoretical issues to practice: "The linguistic terms about phonology would not make any sense to me unless I analysed the different English accents on a cassette as my project work." Trainees also valued opportunities to express themselves creatively, for example, by making posters and doing presentations. As one trainee wrote, "it is fun to do project works because I can use my creativity in designing a poster on morphology or making a teaching resource about syntax."

Many trainees also commented on the fact that the course was conducted in a positive atmosphere, free of the stresses they commonly associate with academic study. The word *fun* occurred frequently in their comments, for example: "I wait for the next linguistics class day because I know that I will have fun!" Some trainees also saw implications for their teaching by looking at the way the course was taught. The following comment reflects a growing understanding of the benefits of choosing topics related to the learners' interests (something I did as much as possible on the linguistics course):

> I'd prepare activities or tasks that are related to students' interests and level. For example, boys like football very much. And one day, I'd prepare an activity related to football. And the other day I'd prepare an activity related to astrology. This activity is liked by girls. Or another option is an activity which is loved by both girls and boys. For example, both girls and boys love "love affairs" and such an activity can be given to them. If they like the topic, they achieve most of the activities. And the more they achieve, the more they are motivated.

Trainees' overall views of the course then, as indicated through their end-of-course evaluations, were very positive. Many of the features I had built into our work and which were based on MI theory, created for the trainees a learning experience which they found more enjoyable, meaningful, and motivating.

Reflection

As a researcher, I had some background information on MIT before I carried out this study. Yet, I had not previously designed a course based on MIT. This study was new to me in that respect. It was also new to me in the sense that it was the first time I had taught the linguistics course. What I learned is that no undergraduate course is inherently boring, despite the impression my trainees had prior to the course and possibly many teachers of linguistics have of the subject too. I have realised that MIT provides resources through which course content can be brought to life for trainees. I have also become aware that cherishing the hidden potential in each learner and seeking ways of developing that potential can enhance the learner's personal, social, and professional growth.

This experience has also opened my eyes to the way in which, when given the opportunity, trainees are able to take responsibility for their learning and to actually provide teachers with information which guides the selection and design of teaching activities. Of course, in university settings there will often be pre-scribed content which must be covered to fulfil the official syllabus, but within these constraints there is often flexibility in terms of how to cover the material. An awareness of how trainees can inform my choice of instructional strategies is something I will carry forward to future courses. This knowledge will allow me to be more flexible in my choice of instructional methods and materials and allow me to adjust these, being sensitive to trainees' needs and wants. Additionally, I now accept that successful teaching is not about finding the best instructional strategy for all learners but about providing a range of experiences which all learners can benefit from in different ways.

The study did, inevitably, present me with a number of challenges and problems. It took a few weeks for the trainees to adjust to what was for them a new way of learning. Because they were also learning a new subject, the challenge for them was significant. The more introverted trainees found it especially difficult to feel comfortable with an approach to learning which encouraged them to participate actively in group projects and presentations. In the future I will try to prepare the trainees for these new experiences by talking, at the start of the course, about the new method and the nature of the classroom procedures we will use.

Also, as I have already noted, it took much time and energy to select, design, evaluate, and revise the teaching activities and resources. However, the analysis of my observations and of the trainee feedback convinced me that this time was well spent. The integration of MIT into my linguistics course not only enriched my teaching experience but also enhanced trainees' sense of confidence and autonomy. I hope that the account of my work that I have provided here will allow teacher educators interested in MIT to experiment with similar ideas in their own contexts and to experience similar benefits.

Eda Üstünel teaches at Mugla University, Turkey.

CHAPTER 13

Between the Lines: Using Interaction Journals in E-mail Projects (*Germany*)

Karin Vogt

Issue

Every language teacher knows that teaching a language also implies teaching a culture. Language and culture cannot be separated (Kramsch, 1993; 1998) and intercultural communicative competence (Byram, 1997; Byram, Gribkova, & Starkey, 2002; Byram, Nichols, & Stevens, 2001; Corbett, 2003) has become an objective in the foreign language classroom on a European basis since the Council of Europe (2001) laid down plurilingualism and pluriculturalism as the most important objectives of foreign language learning for European Union citizens. Pluricultural competence is defined in the *Common European Framework of Reference for Languages* as the "ability to use languages for the purposes of communication and to take part in intercultural interaction, where a person, viewed as a social agent, has proficiency, of varying degrees, in several languages and experience of several cultures" (Council of Europe, 2001, p. 168). So the importance of intercultural competence cannot be denied; however, challenges arise when it comes to the practice of teaching. How can teachers actually teach intercultural communicative competence and, more specifically, the particular component of intercultural competence?

As a foreign language teacher in the lower and upper secondary levels, I wondered about efficient and motivating ways of teaching culture that would not be restricted to imparting knowledge. I wanted to make a change from the authority of the textbook or of the teacher as an expert in the target cultures and present an opportunity for my learners to learn about culture firsthand and autonomously. I wanted learners to see for themselves how their language affects their message and how they establish relationships with and learn from peers from the target cultures. I also wanted to learn about certain features or aspects of everyday life in these cultures that I would not be familiar with as a nonnative teacher.

With these purposes in mind, I had my learners participate in e-mail projects. The focus of e-mail projects is for learners in different linguistic and cultural environments to develop an understanding of each other by negotiating meaning via e-mail. During a restricted period of time, peers exchange e-mails with personal information but, more importantly, with topical information, and thus they can explore individualized understanding of cultural traits in the target communities (Yoshida, 1996). Because learners engage in actual communication and establish real contacts, they ideally apply their cultural knowledge and skills and further develop positive and open attitudes towards members of different cultural communities. In short, e-mail projects may provide an environment for intercultural learning. When I carried out e-mail projects previously, I felt that I did not have sufficient insight into learners' personal impressions and their intercultural learning processes. This time, two initial questions shaped my inquiry: How can I determine whether intercultural learning has taken place? How can I evaluate the development of intercultural learning within the framework of e-mail projects?

Background Literature

As mentioned previously, I had implemented e-mail projects in my English as a foreign language (EFL) classrooms at different stages and with different learner groups. E-mail communication and other forms of telecollaboration have been studied by scholars for some time now (Eck, Legenhausen, & Wolff, 1995; Müller-Hartmann, 1999; Rautenhaus, 1995; Warschauer, 1996). Telecollaboration was defined by Ware (2005) as "a form of network-based language teaching that links students using Internet-mediated communication tools" (p. 64) and can be used to pursue various educational objectives. Teachers can integrate telecollaborative elements to promote language learning by having learners use the foreign language in an authentic communication situation and thus enhance their communicative competence (Donath, 2000; Eck, Legenhausen, & Wolff, 1994; Kern, 1995; Townshend, 1997). With a focus on the intercultural element of the superordinate goal of intercultural communicative competence, telecollaborative learning environments are thought to promote intercultural learning, leading to a better understanding of others and to increased intercultural competence (Furstenberg, Levet, English, & Maillet, 2001; O'Dowd, 2003; Riel, 2000).

The aspects of computer-mediated communication that are conducive to or hinder intercultural learning have been one focus of research. Christian (1997), in his study of three online exchanges in six U.S. classrooms, identified a particular mode of discourse as a significant factor for learners to be willing to share personal information with their peers. He referred to this mode of communication as "talking writing" (p. 64), which sounds like dialogue, with questions and answers and requests for both elaboration and clarification. It builds on previous talking writing and thus maintains a conversation that may contain humour and slang and that has a playful tone. Although the participants in Christian's study were not foreign language learners, they engaged in intercultural communication in an electronic learning environment that induced them to look at their lives and communities through the eyes of learners from different regions with different cultural frames of reference.

O'Dowd (2003), in his study of five Spanish-British dyads (Spanish learners of English at the University of León and British learners of Spanish at King's College London), identified characteristics of an e-mail exchange that are conducive to intercultural learning. Prominent features in those findings were dialogic interaction, including questions, additional opinions, and analyses; acceptance of the culture; and consideration of the sociopragmatic rules of the foreign language.

Differences in communication style that cannot be overcome represent a major impediment to a successful telecollaborative relationship, as suggested by Belz's (2003) case study of one German student communicating with a U.S. partner. She investigated the semantic resources that undergraduate students used to negotiate emotions, judgements, and evaluations, and concluded that a difference in communication patterns led to tensions in the communication and impeded intercultural learning processes. As Ware (2005) presented in her study of 12 students in Germany communicating with 9 students in the United States, other factors that may lead to limited interaction include different expectations and norms for telecollaboration, social and institutional factors that shape tensions, and individual differences in motivation and use of time.

The effect of malfunctioning e-mail exchanges is far-reaching, as I found out in a previous study (Vogt, 2001). In that study, learners in four upper-secondary EFL classrooms in Germany communicated with other EFL learners from Thailand, South Korea, and Japan. Data from e-mail exchanges and follow-up questionnaires as well as field notes showed that learners in malfunctioning exchanges, in which a personal relationship along with a dialogic interaction could not be established or maintained, tended to be less interested in the target culture as a result, some even running the risk of xenophobic tendencies.

In terms of research methodology, the literature on the use of telecollaboration to study intercultural competence commonly adopts an interpretative approach using triangulated data to arrive at a comprehensive picture of the telecollaborative partnership (e.g., Byram, 1997; Byram et al., 2002; Corbett, 2003). Generally, though, insight into the participants' perspectives on the development of their intercultural competence is not provided. In approaching the current study, therefore, I considered two questions with implications for my chosen research approach: How could one account for the development of intercultural competence from the learners' perspective? And how, at the same time, could teachers help their learners explore their response to the intercultural experience?

My response to these questions was to get the participants to keep interaction journals in which they documented their experiences and thoughts throughout the project. I discuss the way these journals were used in more detail in the next section. In providing a rationale for the use of journal writing as a data collection strategy and learning tool, though, my position is that journals enable the learner to carry on a dialogue between various dimensions of intercultural experience. In the case of e-mail projects, journal writing allows both an exploration of different cultures and an introspective experience that consists of questioning one's own culture, which in turn affects the intercultural communication situation. Holly (1997) defined journals as a personal document that could include factual information and subjective aspects typical of the diary. In this way, a dialogue between objective and subjective views can come into being. Through writing, according to Holly, not only are people able to describe, analyse, or clarify events, but the act of writing may lead to further reflections on experiences and "can deepen awareness, broaden perspective, and increase understanding of experience" (1997, p. 12).

Interaction journals were the key data collection strategy used in this study of intercultural learning, and the purpose of this chapter is to analyse the potential of such journals for initiating and tracing intercultural learning processes in the framework of e-mail projects in the EFL classroom.

Procedures

PARTICIPANTS

In the 2001–2002 academic year, two groups of EFL learners ($n = 46$) at a vocational school in Mainz, Germany, were partnered with students in two undergraduate communication courses at a public Midwestern university in the United States ($n = 57$). The U.S. students (21 years old on average) were enrolled in either international or intercultural communication courses. The German participants were 16- to 20-year-old students of a vocational school (business school) at different levels of education. Of the German students, 27 were in grade 11, preparing for their *Abitur*, the final exam of German high-school education, which enables them to attend university. The remaining 19 were completing their first year of a two-year training course as foreign language assistants. Both groups of German students were majoring in English. All of the students had had six years of English, so their command of the language, albeit varying, was generally at an intermediate level. The two groups of students paired up with U.S. students, and participants interacted on a one-to-one basis. Internet access was provided for all participants.

DATA COLLECTION

The project took approximately 3 months. The e-mail exchange was a required course assignment for learners on both sides of the Atlantic. The expected learning outcomes included a range of applied and theoretical objectives, such as engaging in mediated, international communication for the duration of the project, practicing guided self-analysis and evaluation of their exchanges in the form of an analysis paper (U.S. students) or an interaction journal (German students), and gaining an appreciation for the opportunities and limitations of mediated communication as a means of global communication. For the German participants, improving reading and writing skills and enlarging their vocabulary represented an additional objective. The dyads (some participants had more than one partner) started the project by giving and exchanging personal information to establish a personal relationship as a basis for the working relationship. Bearing in mind the importance of the role of tasks in telecollaboration for initiating intercultural learning processes (Müller-Hartmann, 2000), participants discussed topics they had previously determined in class (German students) or that were part of the course syllabus (U.S. students). The German students were also asked to choose a topic for writing a research paper or giving a presentation, collaborating with their partners as firsthand sources of cultural information. Sample topics were universities in the United States, Silicon Valley, or part-time jobs for students. German participants were asked to compose entries in their interaction journals every time they received e-mail from their U.S. partners. The entry was to comprise a summary of the e-mail received and a reflective part, noting related impressions, feelings, and thoughts. Interaction journals were collected by the teacher at the end of the exchange as a part of the course assignment. The analysis presented here is based on data from the e-mail sent and written by the 46 German learners and from their interaction journals.

DATA ANALYSIS

Interaction journals and e-mails were subject to content analysis, as suggested by Mayring (1999). Qualitative content analysis typically considers the context of text components, takes into account latent meanings, integrates striking individual cases, and incorporates interpretations of elements not directly observable in the text (Mayring, 1995, 1999).

Mayring's (1999) approach to qualitative content analysis involves the development of a system of categories on the basis of text material. The material is dissected and analysed in a sequenced procedure. After summarising the text material, the researcher makes ambiguous or unclear passages comprehensible by using supplementary data, such as other information in the text or information about the subject. In this study, the analysis included e-mails or corresponding data from the U.S. counterparts, such as their analysis papers. Under Mayring's approach, the material is then analysed and structured with regard to the research questions. In this case, analysis and structuring hinged on striking characteristics related to the following categories that, in turn, arose from the research questions:

1. How can interaction journals help teachers trace and describe intercultural learning processes?

2. To what extent are interaction journals suitable as teaching or learning tools?

Results

INTERCULTURAL LEARNING PROCESSES

Two aspects of intercultural learning highlighted in the interaction journals are considered here. One relates to the way that new cultural information and awareness was obtained; the other relates to the way that learners were moved to view their own cultures from the perspective of an outsider.

Stimulating Cultural Insights

The data highlight ways in which intercultural learning was often stimulated when one partner volunteered cultural information that sparked interest in the other. One example from an interaction journal shows that the personal information one partner gave the interlocutor incited her to find out more about the cultural trait itself, namely lacrosse as an example of a team sport that is widely popular in North America but hardly known in Germany. The interaction journal contained the following entry:

> In addition to that I get the information that she lived in Ohio for 11 years. Furthermore she [is] involved [in] a sport team. The sport which she do is called lacrosse. I can't imagine what kind of sport this is and I asked her to explain me this kind of sport.

The German partner decided to ask for clarification concerning the sport. When she received the required information, her interest was aroused and she wanted to find out even more about it independent of her partner's interest in it:

In her e-mail she answers my questions what lacrosse is. Anne explains that lacrosse has 12 team members on the field at one time. They have a goalie that is covered with equipment and a stick. The rest of the team just wears kilts, t-shirts and a mouthguard. The stick is smaller than the goalies. The point of the game is to score a goal on a square goal. The highest score wins. . . . I find that Anne has my question what lacrosse is very good explaines. Now I can imagine what kind of sport it is. I am very interested in this sport and would like to see it live.

The entries in the interaction journal thus helped the teacher find instances of an attitude of openness and curiosity, an important aspect of intercultural competence (Byram, 1997), apart from the cultural knowledge that the partner gained. A different dyad exchanged information on Halloween. The U.S. partner casually referred to a Halloween party she and a friend had given in their house. Again, the entry in the German interaction journal shows that this learner acquired cultural knowledge by processing individualised information but also increased his or her cultural awareness in the process:

Moira told me how they had celebrated Halloween. They had a big party in their house and decorated much with pumpkins and other shocking things. People came costumed the best costumed person got a prize and it was much fun. . . . I think it's good that we write each other about the differents between the U.S. and Germany. So you know that it can be very different from your place to another. We don't celebrate Halloween as much as the people do in the U.S. I know that before but I don't know the details how they celebrate it. It's very interesting for me to know.

Changing Intercultural Perspectives

As noted previously, an open and curious attitude towards otherness is conducive to intercultural learning. In connection with attitudes as a part of intercultural communicative competence, Byram (1997) also mentioned that interlocutors need to learn to decentre. In other words, by not regarding their own culture as the norm but as one option out of many, learners might avoid a potentially ethnocentric perspective. Intercultural learning processes are thus also characterised by an attempt to relativise one's own perspective by trying to see things, including those related to the learner's own culture, from a different perspective. The ability to step back and look at things from a previously unfamiliar perspective is a great challenge. But this approach is necessary to cultural understanding and conducive to raising awareness about one's own cultural environment that "allows a conscious control of biased interpretation" (Byram, 1997, p. 35).

The interaction journals also provided insights into how e-mail exchanges led learners to relativise their views in the way described previously. One dyad from the exchange compared the legal age for drinking in both countries. The German partner wrote the following entry in her interaction journal after the discussion:

> Furthermore, I am informed, that people are able to drink alcohol legally when they turn 21. I think that law is [better] as in Germany. In my opinion people in the age of 16 or 17 drinks too much alcohol without seeing the consequent. Some people in Germany think that they cant have a party without alcohol. They argues that they cant have fun without alcohol. But in my opinion that is a completely silly argument.

The learner displayed her ability to decentre when she did not take the beliefs underlying the legislation in her culture to be superior. She acknowledged that other interpretations of the law might make better sense, starting from critical observations on her own environment.

In the next example from an interaction journal, the interlocutor started from the assumption that her partner was not very familiar with the cultural concept she was trying to mediate in her e-mail, namely Carnival. Mainz is one of the most important and active cities in Germany during Carnival season, which begins in November and ends on Ash Wednesday each year. Learners in the Mainz area get two or three days' holiday and many businesses remain closed for the Carnival parade. Numerous learners play an active part in Carnival clubs. The interlocutor from Mainz looked at the event through the eyes of her partner and thus decentred. In her interaction journal, she related what she included in her e-mail about Carnival, or Fasching:

> Today I wrote a mail to Sonny. I informed him about the Carnival time, which started and that we [don't have to] go to school for two days. I explained him in a short text what Fasching is and how it is celebrate, Additional I sent him three pictures of Carnival. I hope these pictures give him an idea what our Fasching looks like.

This learner understood that what is familiar to her is not necessarily familiar to her partner, so she made an effort not only to explain the special concept from her culture and region, but also to illustrate it with photos she found on the Internet.

These examples illustrate how participants in an e-mail project manage to decentre, step back from their own cultural frame of reference, and eventually change perspectives. I found several instances in the data of learners taking the first steps towards decentring and thus advancing their intercultural learning processes. There were frequent instances of partners who were surprised on hearing information that they had not anticipated at all. Interestingly, these instances often related to perceptions of their culture by others. The German partner in the next example asked her e-mail partner how Germans were perceived in her community. She was taken aback at the answer, as reflected in the journal entry:

> She replied [to] my question what Americans actually thought about us. Well, in her opinion it depends on the person, but although she hate to admit it, she mentioned that Germany was connected with Adolf Hitler. This is one aspect I've never thought of. Surely, it belongs to our history, but I believed that they consider this as past.

The honest answer her interlocutor provided was eye-opening for this German learner, because through it she was confronted with a discrepancy between her views of her culture and those of others.

Another example shows how learners were incited to question their familiar assumptions and how formerly normal aspects were viewed differently in relation to their partner's comments: "I did not know that German enterprises are known for the ample vacation time they give to the employees." During the exchange of the same dyad, the German participant was asked about stereotypes by her interlocutor. As the journal entry shows, she had never actually thought about that issue.

> I have to think about the stereotypes Germans have of Americans because I have no idea at the moment. My opinion is that every stereotype has something true [in it]. For example no one can dispute that many Germans love to drink beer.

Giving an undifferentiated statement at first, she then admits that she would need to take some time to reflect on heterostereotypes, which then leads to a reflection of heterostereotypes other cultural groups hold of Germans. This can be interpreted as a first step towards cultural awareness because it includes an awareness of a variety of often conflicting images and perceptions.

INTERACTION JOURNALS AS TEACHING OR LEARNING TOOLS

I comment here on two ways in which the interaction journals supported teaching and learning. Firstly, they highlighted for the teacher aspects of intercultural learning that could provide the basis of classroom activities. Secondly, they provided learners with a means to reflect on the nature of the interaction with their partners.

Interaction Journal Data as the Basis of Teaching

In many cases the data in the journals identified potential learning opportunities that the German interlocutors did not explore further with their partners. These entries suggested issues that I could encourage my learners to consider as part of their intercultural learning. For example, one learner commented in her journal on the fact that her U.S. partner shared a whole house with her fellow students: "It surprises me that Dora lives in a house. I never heard that a student can afford to live in a house even if he shares it with his roommates." In this case, the learner interpreted the information on the basis of her own cultural frame of reference, transferring the student housing situation she was familiar with from her own environment to that of her partner. Mainz is a university town, but one where detached houses can only be afforded by families and professionals, and students either live in halls or share flats. The learner did not explore this further with her partner, and therefore the teacher used this issue as the basis of in-class discussion to encourage greater awareness and understanding of this particular cultural difference.

The interaction journals also revealed instances in which learners documented thoughts they had not raised in e-mails with their partners for fear of creating tensions or misunderstandings. Again, such issues provided starting points for class discussions, which furthered learners' intercultural awareness. In one example, a learner received information from her partner on her research topic, namely universities in the United States. This is how she reacted to the information she was given about Ivy League schools, which she had not heard of before:

> Kyra told me something about "Yale," "Harvard" and "BGSU" [the partner university]. Yale and Harvard are called Ivy League Schools and are very expensive and very hard to get into. There you have to have perfect grades and an impressive extra-curricular list. But when you go to one of these schools and you have good marks then you often have an easier time to get a well-paid job. At schools like Bowling Green State University you get into much easier. I don't understand why somebody [would] pay so much money for a school.

Her comment in the last sentence has to be attributed to the fact that she was accustomed to the concept of free education in Germany along with an egalitarian approach to education in which the public universities do not levy fees and are not grouped into different categories. A potential incident could have occurred if she had voiced her lack of sympathy in the direct way that some Germans are known for. If such an incident had occurred, it could have been taken up as a stimulus for intercultural learning processes in the classroom. Apart from cultural knowledge that could be built up—possibly by others in the group who have a clearer notion of the concept of Ivy League Schools—the underlying difference in beliefs and values in educational systems could be clarified by putting them in a historical context. Thus the discussion could also shed light on the learners' cultural environment, which could help them raise their awareness of their own cultures.

The interaction journals provided a basis of classroom work when they documented critical incidents, such as disagreements or tensions that the German learners experienced during the e-mail projects. For example, during the U.S. spring break, one German partner's interlocutor was not available for information on the learner's research task. The German learner expressed her dissatisfaction in her interaction journal: "I think it is unfair that she wouldn't write to me while she is in Cancun when I need the information now. She could get to an Internet café."

This highly insensitive entry (given that she herself did not write to her partner during her own holidays in Poland) could (when anonymised) form the basis of an in-class discussion of learners' expectations of their partners and possible divergences of expectations (see also Ware, 2005). It could also be used for a role-play activity designed to see the matter through her partner's eyes: Would the partner go to an Internet café to complete a school assignment during her holidays abroad? Exploring such incidents might actually change perspectives and increase learners' empathy.

Interaction Journals as Learning Tools: Dialogic Interaction

The dialogic aspect of intercultural communication situations has been underlined by Christian (1997), O'Dowd (2003), and others as being a prerequisite for successful communication. Interaction journals are suitable learning tools because they allow participants to evaluate the quality of their dialogic communication and to assess the success of the interaction at different stages. An entry from the beginning of one exchange illustrates this: "Maria had a lot of questions for me, that showed me that she is interested in doing this project with me." By analysing her partner's communication style in her reply, the learner tried to gauge her partner's interest in the project as a precondition for its success. Another learner, also at the beginning of a project, went into great detail analysing his partner's first e-mail in the interaction journal:

> My first impression is very well, because Marc sounds very friendly and shows his interest to the e-mail project. The first question to me shows that he wants contact with me. The 2nd question in the 3rd paragraph was a connection to the mail which I had sent him before. So, he makes clear that he had received the letter and now he wants to know something more about what I had written.

The learner analysed the e-mail for hints of a dialogic interaction, particularly for instances of reciprocity in discourse. From this, he inferred the intensity of his partner's interest in the exchange. He indirectly anticipated the probability of success for the exchange.

In the case of failing interaction, interaction journals can serve as an outlet for disappointment and as a place where learners can analyse the reasons for the failure, as illustrated by a series of entries from one learner. From the beginning, the exchange did not seem to take off, at least in her view: "In my opinion [he] did not write much and he did not answer all my question. For the first mail it was OK, but I was a bit disappointed." In an entry she wrote in the course of this fairly unsuccessful interaction, she tried to evaluate the quality of the exchange in terms of dialogic interaction: "He didn't write much, like in his first mail. It is sad, because I always write a lot and I ask a lot of questions. But Fred simply doesn't answer them. What shall I do?" Her question showed that she was at a loss regarding what to do. Her analysis of the previous e-mails showed which aspects she regarded as essential for a successful interaction, namely providing substantial information herself and initiating talking writing by getting back to the partner's questions and comments.

Entries in interaction journals also provided insights into how participants actively constructed interaction in a systematic way, for example, by planning their responses. In one example, a learner referred to a hobby that her partner had mentioned: "Some hobbies of Bree are needlepointing and drawing houses. But I don't have a clue what needlepointing is. So, I'll ask her in the next e-mail." The partner consciously planned her response; in doing so, she would not only deepen her intercultural learning but also enhance the interaction with her partner.

By studying learners' interaction journals I became aware of how learners reflected on, assessed, and tried to manage the dialogic interaction with their partners. This awareness was valuable for me in identifying aspects of intercultural learning to focus on in my work with these learners.

Reflection

The purpose of this study was to explore, in the context of research on e-mail projects, the ways interaction journals help teachers trace and describe intercultural learning processes and to evaluate the suitability of interaction journals as a teaching or learning tool. My analysis of interaction journals from two e-mail projects in my classroom has reinforced my belief in the value of such journals for teachers and learners. The insights that I gained into my learners' lives and thoughts were extremely helpful for me as a teacher; they allowed me to enhance the quality of teacher-learner relationships in my classes and to better understand more generally the issues my learners might respond to positively in language learning tasks. For learners, the interaction journals provided room for them to reflect on the quality of dialogic interaction as presented in the interaction.

Interaction journals also have great potential as teaching tools. Although I have not fully exploited this function in my teaching, I certainly should. Several kinds of data from the journal suggested material for profitable classroom discussions. Sometimes this material stemmed from differences between the cultures of the partners; at other times it derived from misunderstandings or tensions that arose during the e-mail exchanges and that learners then reflected on.

This study also confirmed my view that the teacher plays a central role in managing and monitoring telecollaborative learning environments. Especially when using entries in interaction journals as a teaching tool, it became clear to me again how much the teacher is in demand to initiate, plan, and monitor intercultural learning processes. The teacher must play a central role not only in setting up opportunities for intercultural communication but also in supporting learners in such a way that those opportunities promote intercultural learning in a productive and positive manner.

Karin Vogt teaches at the University of Education, Karlsruhe, Germany.

References

Abelson, R. (1979). Differences between belief systems and knowledge systems. *Cognitive Science, 3,* 355–366.

Allen, P., Fröhlich, M., & Spada, N. (1984). The communicative orientation of language teaching: An observation scheme. In J. Handscombe, R. A. Orem, & B. P. Taylor (Eds.), *On TESOL '83: The question of control* (pp. 231–253). Alexandria, VA: TESOL.

Allwright, D., & Bailey, K. (1991). *Focus on the language classroom.* Cambridge, England: Cambridge University Press.

Altman, H. B., & James, C. V. (Eds.). (1980). *Foreign language teaching: Meeting individual needs.* Oxford, England: Pergamon.

Altrichter, H., Posch, P., & Somekh, B. (1993). *Teachers investigate their work.* London: Routledge.

Alvarado, C. (1992). Discourse style and patterns of participation on ESL interactive tasks. *TESOL Quarterly 26,* 589–593.

Appel, J. (1995). *Diary of a language teacher.* Oxford, England: Heinemann.

Armstrong, T. (1987). Describing strengths in children identified as "learning disabled" using Howard Gardner's theory of multiple intelligences as an organising framework. *Dissertation Abstracts International, 48,* 08A. (University Microfilms No. 87–25, 844)

Armstrong, T. (1988). Learning differences—not disabilities. *Principal, 68*(1), 34–36.

Armstrong, T. (1994*). Multiple intelligences in the classroom.* Alexandria, VA: Association for Supervision and Curriculum Development.

Arnold, J. (Ed.). (1999). *Affect in language learning*. Cambridge, England: Cambridge University Press.

Bailey, K. M. (1990). The use of diary studies in teacher education programs. In J. C. Richards & D. Nunan (Eds.), *Second language teacher education* (pp. 43–61). New York: Cambridge University Press.

Bailey, K. M. (2001). Observation. In R. Carter & D. Nunan (Eds.), *The Cambridge guide to teaching English to speakers of other languages* (pp. 114–119). Cambridge, England: Cambridge University Press.

Bailey, K. M., Curtis, A., & Nunan, D. (1998). Undeniable insights: The collaborative use of three professional development practices. *TESOL Quarterly, 32,* 546–556.

Bandura, A. (1977). Self-efficacy: Toward a unifying theory of behavioural change. *Psychological Review, 41,* 191–215.

Bandura, A. (1986). *Social foundations of thought and action: A social cognitive theory.* Englewood Cliffs, NJ: Prentice Hall.

Barnes, D. (1976). *From communication to curriculum.* Harmondsworth, England: Penguin.

Barth, R. S. (1990). *Improving schools from within.* San Francisco: Jossey-Bass.

Beaumont, M., & O'Brien, T. (2000). *Collaborative research in second language education.* Stoke on Trent, England: Trentham Books.

Belz, J. (2003). Linguistic perspectives on the development of intercultural competence in telecollaboration. *Language Learning & Technology, 7*(2), 68–117.

Benson, A., & Blackman, D. (2003). Can research methods ever be interesting? *Active Learning in Higher Education, 4,* 39–55.

Bhattacharyya, G., Ison, L., & Blair, M. (2003). *Minority ethnic attainment and participation in education and training* (Department for Education and Skills [DfES] Report, Research Topic Paper RTP01-03). Nottingham, England: DfES.

Biber, D., & Conrad, S. (2001). Quantitative corpus-based research: Much more than bean counting. *TESOL Quarterly, 35,* 331–336.

Birbili, M. (2003). *Teaching educational research methods.* Retrieved July 17, 2006, from http://escalate.ac.uk/1055

Black, S. (1996, March). Redefining the teacher's role. *Executive Educator, 18*(8), 23–26.

Borg, S. (2001). The research journal: A tool for promoting and understanding researcher development. *Language Teaching Research, 5,* 156–177.

Bourdieu, P. (2001). Language and symbolic power. In A. Javorsky & N. Coupland (Eds.), *The Discourse Reader* (pp. 502–513). London: Routledge.

Bowler, B., & Parminter, S. (1993). *Making headway: Literature (upper intermediate).* Oxford, England: Oxford University Press.

Britton, J. (1994). Vygotsky's contribution to pedagogical theory. In S. Brindley (Ed.), *Teaching English* (pp. 259–263). London: Routledge.

Brown, H. D. (1994). *Teaching by principles: An interactive approach to language pedagogy.* Englewood Cliffs, NJ: Prentice Hall.

Brown, J., & Hudson, T. (1998). The alternatives in language assessment. *TESOL Quarterly, 32,* 653–675.

Brumfit, C. J. (1984). *Communicative methodology in language teaching.* Cambridge, England: Cambridge University Press.

Brumfit, C. J., & Carter, R. (1986). *Literature and language teaching.* Oxford, England: Oxford University Press.

Buchberger, F., & Byrne, K. (1995). Quality in teacher education: A suppressed theme? *European Journal of Teacher Education, 18,* 9–23.

Burns, A. (1999). *Collaborative action research for English language teachers.* Cambridge, England: Cambridge University Press.

Bygate, M., Skehan, P., & Swain, M. (Eds.). (2001). *Researching pedagogic tasks.* Hemel Hempstead, England: Pearson.

Byram, M. (1997). *Teaching and assessing intercultural communicative competence.* Clevedon, England: Multilingual Matters.

Byram, M., Gribkova, B., & Starkey, H. (2002). *Developing the intercultural dimension in language teaching. A practical introduction for teachers.* Strasbourg, France: Council of Europe.

Byram, M., Nichols, A., & Stevens, D. (Eds.). (2001). *Developing intercultural competence in practice.* Clevedon, England: Multilingual Matters.

Campbell, A., McNamara, O., & Gilroy, P. (2004). *Practitioner research and professional development in education.* London: Paul Chapman.

Campbell, L. (1997, September). Variations on a theme: How teachers interpret MI theory. *Educational Leadership, 55*(1), 15–19.

Campbell, L., & Campbell, B. (1999*). Multiple intelligences and student achievement: Success stories from six schools.* Alexandria, VA: Association for Supervision and Curriculum Development.

Campbell, L., Campbell, B., & Dickinson, D. (1996). *Teaching and learning through multiple intelligences.* Needham, MA: Allyn & Bacon.

Canale, M., & Swain, M. (1980). Theoretical bases of communicative approaches to second language teaching and testing. *Applied Linguistics 1,* 1–47.

Cardoza, L. (1994). Getting a word in edgewise: Does "not talking" mean "not learning"? *TESOL Journal, 4*(1), 24–27.

Carter, R., & McRae, J. (Eds.). (1996). *Language, literature, and the learner: Creative classroom practice.* Amsterdam: Longman.

Cederblom, J., & Paulsen, D. W. (2001). *Critical reasoning: Understanding and criticising arguments and theories.* Belmont, CA: Wadsworth/Thomson Learning.

Chapman, C. (1993). *If the shoe fits . . . How to develop multiple intelligences in the classroom.* Palatine, IL: IRI/Skylight.

Chaudron, C. (1988). *Second language classrooms: Research on teaching and learning.* Cambridge, England: Cambridge University Press.

Chen, J., Belkada, S., & Okamoto, T. (2004). How a Web-based course facilitates acquisition of English for academic purposes. *Language Learning & Technology, 8*(2), 33–49. Retrieved May 17, 2006, from http://llt.msu.edu/vol8num2/chen/default.html

Christian, S. (1997). *Exchanging lives: Middle school writers online*. Urbana, IL: National Council of Teachers of English.

Christison, M. (1997). An introduction to multiple intelligences theory and second language learning. In J. Reid (Eds.), *Understanding learning styles in the second language classroom* (pp. 1–14). Englewood Cliffs, NJ: Prentice Hall/Regents.

Christison, M. (1998). Applying multiple intelligences theory in preservice and inservice TEFL education programs. *English Teaching Forum, 36*(2), 2–13.

Christison, M. (1999, September/October). Multiple intelligences: Teaching the whole student. *ESL Magazine, 2*, 10–13.

Christison, M. (2001*). Applying multiple intelligences theory in the second and foreign language classroom*. Burlingame, CA: Alta Book Center.

Cochran-Smith, M., & Lytle, S. L. (1990). Research on teaching and teacher research: The issues that divide. *Educational Researcher, 19*(2), 2–11.

Cochran-Smith, M., & Lytle, S. L. (1999). The teacher research movement: A decade later. *Educational Researcher, 28*(7), 15–25.

Collie, J., & Porter-Ladousse, G. (1991). *Paths into poetry*. Oxford, England: Oxford University Press.

Collie, J., & Slater, S. (1998). *Short stories for creative language*. Cambridge, England: Cambridge University Press.

Connor, H., La Valle, I., Tackey, N. D., & Perryman, S. (1996). *Ethnic minority graduates: Differences by degrees* (Institute for Employment Studies Report 309). Brighton, England: Institute for Employment Studies.

Connor, H., Tyers, C., Davis, S., Tackey, N. D., & Modood, T. (2003). *Minority ethnic students in higher education: Interim report* (DfES Research Report RR448). Nottingham, England: DfES.

Corbett, J. (2003). *An intercultural approach to English language teaching*. Clevedon, England: Multilingual Matters.

Corden, R. (1992). The role of the teacher. In K. Norman (Ed.), *Thinking voices: The work of the National Oracy Project* (pp. 172–185). London: Hodder and Stoughton.

Council of Europe. (2001). *Common European Framework of Reference for Languages: Learning, teaching, assessment*. Cambridge, England: Cambridge University Press.

Crookes, G., & Schmidt, R. (1991). Motivation: Reopening the research agenda. *Language Learning, 41*, 469–512.

Cumming, A., Shi, L., & So, S. (1997). Learning to do research on language teaching and learning: Graduate apprenticeships. *System 25*, 425–433.

Cunningham, S., & Moor, P. (1998). *Cutting edge intermediate teacher's resource book*. Harlow, England: Longman.

Darling-Hammond, L. (2003, May). Keeping good teachers: Why it matters, what leaders can do. *Educational Leadership, 60*(8), 6–13.

Davies, P. (1999). What is evidence-based education? *British Journal of Educational Studies, 47*(2), 108–121.

Day, C. (1984). Teachers' thinking, intentions, and practice: An action research perspective. In R. Halkes & J. Olson (Eds.), *Teacher thinking* (pp. 7–18). Lisse, the Netherlands: Swets & Zeitlinger.

Deci, E. L., Pelletier, L. G., Ryan, R. M., & Vallerand, R. J. (1991). Motivation and education: The self-determination perspective. *Educational Psychologist, 26,* 325–346.

Deci, E. L., & Ryan, R. M. (1985). *Intrinsic motivation and self-determination in human behavior.* New York: Plenum Press.

Deem, R., & Lucas, L. (2002, December). *Learning about research: Some reflections on the teaching/research relationship.* Paper presented at the Society for Research in Higher Education Conference, Glasgow, Scotland.

Donath, R. (2000). Electronic-mail im fremdsprachenunterricht: Da geht die post ab [Electronic mail in the foreign language classroom—to the four corners of the world]. In R. Donath & I. Volkmer (Eds.), *Das transatlantische klassenzimmer* (2nd ed., pp. 123–136). Hamburg, Germany: Körber-Stiftung.

Dörnyei, Z. (2003). Attitudes, orientations, and motivations in language learning: Advances in theory, research, and applications. *Language Learning, 53*(Supplement 1), 3–32.

Doughty, C., & Pica, T. (1986). "Information gap" tasks: Do they facilitate second language acquisition? *TESOL Quarterly, 20,* 305–325.

Duff, A., & Maley, A. (1990). *Literature.* Oxford, England: Oxford University Press.

Duffy, T. M., & Jonassen, D. H. (1992). *Constructivism and the technology of instruction: A conversation.* Hillsdale, NJ: Lawrence Erlbaum.

Eck, A., Legenhausen, L., & Wolff, D. (1994). Telekommunikation als werkzeug zur gestaltung einer spracherwerbsfördernden lernumgebung: Möglichkeiten und probleme [Telecommunication as a tool for a learning environment conducive to language acquisition: Possibilities and problems]. In J. Fechner (Ed.), *Neue wege im computergestützten fremdsprachenunterricht* (pp. 59–74). Berlin, Germany: Langenscheidt.

Eck, A., Legenhausen, L., & Wolff, D. (1995). *Telekommunikation und fremdsprachenunterricht: Informationen, projekte, ergebnisse* [Telecommunication and foreign language learning: Information, projects, results]. Bochum, Germany: AKS.

Edge, J. (2001). Attitude and access: Building a new teaching/learning community in TESOL. In J. Edge (Ed.), *Action research* (pp. 1–11). Alexandria, VA: TESOL.

Egan, G. (2000). *The skilled helper: A problem management approach to helping* (7th ed.). Pacific Grove, CA: Brooks/Cole.

Ellis, C., & Sinclair, B. (1989). *Learning to learn English.* Cambridge, England: Cambridge University Press.

Ellis, R. (1994). *The study of second language acquisition.* Oxford, England: Oxford University Press.

Ellis, R. (2003). *Task-based language learning and teaching.* Oxford, England: Oxford University Press.

Felix, U. (2001). A multivariate analysis of students' experience of Web-based learning. *Australian Journal of Educational Technology, 17,* 21–36.

Fleming, N. (2006). *VARK: A guide to learning styles.* Retrieved May 22, 2006, from http://www.vark-learn.com/english/index.asp

Ford, M. E. (1992). *Motivating humans: Goals, emotions, and personal agency beliefs.* Newbury Park, CA: Sage.

Francis, S., Hirsch, S., & Rowland, E. (1994). Improving school culture through study groups. *Journal of Staff Development, 13*(2), 12–15.

Freeman, D. (1989). Teacher training, development, and decision making: A model of teaching and related strategies for language teacher education. *TESOL Quarterly, 23,* 27–46.

Freeman, D. (1998). *Doing teacher research.* Boston: Heinle & Heinle.

Furstenberg, G., Levet, S., English, K., & Maillet, K. (2001). Giving a virtual voice to the silent language of culture: The cultura project. *Language Learning & Technology, 5*(1), 55–102.

Gardner, H. (1983). *Frames of mind: The theory of multiple intelligences.* New York: Basic Books.

Gardner, H. (1993). Educating for understanding. *The American School Board Journal, 180,* 20–24.

Gardner, H. (1995). Reflections on multiple intelligences: Myths and messages. *Phi Delta Kappan, 77,* 200–208.

Gardner, H. (1997). Six afterthoughts: Comments on varieties of intellectual talent. *Journal of Creative Behavior, 31,* 120–124.

Gardner, H., & Hatch, T. (1989). Multiple intelligences go to school. *Educational Researcher, 18*(8), 4–9.

Gardner, R. C. (1985). *Social psychological aspects of second language learning.* London: Arnold.

Gardner, R. C., & MacIntyre, P. D. (1992). A student's contributions to second language learning. Part I: Cognitive variables. *Language Teaching, 25,* 211–220.

Gardner, R. C., & MacIntyre, P. D. (1993). A student's contributions to second language learning. Part II: Affective variables. *Language Teaching, 26,* 1–11.

Gebhard, J. G. (1999). Reflecting through a teaching journal. In J. G. Gebhard & R. Oprandy, *Language teaching awareness*: *A guide to exploring beliefs and practices* (pp. 78–98). Cambridge, England: Cambridge University Press.

Gebhard, J. G., & Oprandy, R. (1999). *Language teaching awareness*: *A guide to exploring beliefs and practices.* Cambridge, England: Cambridge University Press.

Goswami, D., & Stillman, P. (1987). *Reclaiming the classroom: Teacher research as an agency for change.* Portsmouth, NH: Boynton Cook.

Granger, S. (1998). *Learner English on computer.* London: Longman.

Granger, S., Hung, J., & Petch-Tyson, S. (Eds.) (2002). *Computer learner corpora: Second language acquisition and foreign language teaching.* Amsterdam: John Benjamins.

Hancock, M. (1997). Behind classroom code switching: Layering and language choice in L2 learner interaction. *TESOL Quarterly, 31,* 217–235.

Harlow, L. L. (1987). Individualized instruction in foreign languages at the college level: A survey of programs in the United States. *Modern Language Journal, 7,* 389–394.

Harris, M. (1996). *Review of postgraduate education* (Higher Education Funding Council for England [HEFCE] M 14/96). Bristol, England: HEFCE, Committee of Vice-Chancellors and Principals and Standing Committee of Principals.

Head, K., & Taylor, P. (1997). *Readings in teacher development*. London: Heinemann.

Heyworth, F. (2004). Why the CEF is important. In K. Morrow (Ed.), *Insights from the Common European Framework* (pp. 12–21). Oxford, England: Oxford University Press.

Hill, J. (1986). *Using literature in language teaching*. London: McMillan.

Hoerr, T. R. (1996a). Focusing on the personal intelligences as a basis for success. *NASSP Bulletin, 80*(583), 36–42.

Hoerr, T. R. (1996b). Introducing the theory of multiple intelligences. *NASSP Bulletin, 80*(583), 8–10.

Holly, M. L. (1997). *Keeping a professional journal* (2nd ed.). Sydney, Australia: University of New South Wales Press.

Hopkins, D. (1985). *A teacher's guide to classroom research*. Milton Keynes, England: Open University Press.

Horwitz, E. K. (1987). Surveying student beliefs about language learning. In A. Wenden & J. Rubin (Eds.), *Learning strategies in language learning* (pp. 119–129). Englewood Cliffs, NJ: Prentice Hall.

Huberman, M. (1996). Moving mainstream: Taking a closer look at teacher research. *Language Arts, 73*, 124–140.

Huerta-Macias, A. (1995). Alternative assessment: Responses to commonly asked questions. *TESOL Journal, 5*(1), 8–11.

Hunston, S. (2002). *Corpora in applied linguistics*. Cambridge, England: Cambridge University Press.

Hutchinson, T., & Waters, A. (1987). *English for specific purposes: A learning-centred approach*. Cambridge, England: Cambridge University Press.

Jarvis, H. (2001). Internet usage of English for academic purposes courses. *ReCALL, 13*, 206–212.

Jarvis, H. (2004). Investigating the blended applications of computers on EFL courses at higher education institutions in UK. *Journal of English for Academic Purposes, 3*, 111–137.

Jarvis, J. (1992). Using diaries for teacher reflection on in-service courses. *ELT Journal, 46*, 133–143.

Johns, B. (1996). Interview with Henry G. Widdowson. *GRETA, 4*(2), 36–43.

Johns, T. (1994). From printout to handout: Grammar and vocabulary teaching in the context of data-driven learning. In T. Odlin (Ed.), *Perspectives on pedagogical grammar* (pp. 293–313). Cambridge, England: Cambridge University Press.

Johnson, D. W., & Johnson, R. T. (1991). *Learning together and alone*. Boston: Allyn & Bacon.

Jonassen, D. H., Ambruso, D. R., & Olesen, J. (1992). Designing a hypertext on transfusion medicine using cognitive flexibility theory. *International Journal of Educational Multimedia and Hypermedia, 1*, 309–322.

Kagan, S. (1992). *Cooperative learning*. San Juan de Capistrano, CA: Kagan Cooperative Learning.

Kemmis, S., & McTaggart, R. (Eds.). (1992). *The action research planner* (3rd ed.). Geelong, Victoria, Australia: Deakin University Press.

Kern, R. (1995). Restructuring classroom interaction with networked computers: Effects on quality and quantity of language production. *Modern Language Journal, 79*, 457–476.

Kiely, R., Clibbon, G., Rea-Dickins, P., Walter, C., & Woodfield, H. (2004). *Teachers into researchers*. London: CILT. Retrieved May 12, 2006, from http://www.bris.ac.uk/education/research/centres/creole/projects/reportir

Knight, S., & Boudah, D. (1998, April). *Participatory research and development*. Paper presented at the annual meeting of the American Educational Research Association, San Diego, CA.

Knodt, J. S. (1997, September). A think tank cultivates kids. *Educational Leadership, 55*(1), 35–37.

Kraft, N. P. (2002). Teacher research as a way to engage in critical reflection: A case study. *Reflective Practice, 3*, 176–190.

Kramsch, C. (1993). *Context and culture in language teaching*. Oxford, England: Oxford University Press.

Kramsch, C. (1998). *Language and culture*. Oxford, England: Oxford University Press.

Krashen, S., & Terrell, T. (1983). *The natural approach: Language acquisition in the classroom*. Oxford, England: Pergamon Press.

Lankshear, C., & Knobel, M. (2004). *A handbook for teacher research: From design to implementation*. Berkshire, England: Open University Press.

Larsen-Freeman, D. (2000). *Techniques and principles in language teaching*. New York: Oxford University Press.

Latham, A. S. (1997, September). Quantifying MI's gains. *Educational Leadership, 55*(1), 84–85.

Lazar, G. (1993). *Literature and language teaching*. Cambridge, England: Cambridge University Press.

Lazear, D. (1991). *Seven ways of teaching: The artistry of teaching with multiple intelligences*. Palantine, IL: IRI/Skylight.

Lewin, K. (1946a). Action research and minority problems. *Journal of Social Issues, 2*, 34–46.

Lewin, K. (1946b). Action research and minority problems. In G. W. Lewin (Ed.), *Resolving social conflicts*. New York: Harper & Row.

Lewis, H. (1990). *A question of values*. San Francisco: Harper & Row.

Lieberman, A., & Miller, L. (Eds.). (2001). *Teachers caught in the action: Professional development that matters*. New York: Teachers College Press.

Little, J. W. (1993). Professional community in comprehensive high schools: The two worlds of academic and vocational teachers. In J. Little & M. McLaughlin (Eds.), *Teacher's work: Individuals, colleagues, and contexts* (pp. 137–163). New York: Teachers College Press.

Littlejohn, A. (1996). What is a good task? *English Teaching Professional, 1*, 2–3.

Long, M. H. (1981). Input, interaction, and second language acquisition. In H. Winitz (Ed.), *Native language and foreign language acquisition: Annals of the New York Academy of Sciences, 379* (pp. 259–278). New York: New York Academy of Sciences.

Long, M. H. (1983). Linguistic and conversational adjustments to nonnative speakers. *Studies in Second Language Acquisition, 5,* 177–193.

Loucks-Horsley, S., Hewson, P., Love, P., & Stiles, K. (1998). *Designing professional development for teachers of science and mathematics.* Thousand Oaks, CA: Corwin Press.

Lytle, S. L., & Cochran-Smith, M. (1990). Learning from teacher research: A working typology. *Teachers College Record, 92*(1), 83–103.

Maley, A. (1994). *Short and sweet: Short texts and how to use them.* London: Penguin Books.

Maley, A. (2001). Literature in the language classroom. In R. Carter & D. Nunan (Eds.), *The Cambridge guide to teaching English to speakers of other languages* (pp. 180–185). Cambridge, England: Cambridge University Press.

Marzano, R., Brandt, R., Hughes, C., Jones, B., Presseisen, B., & Rankin, S. (1988). *Dimensions of thinking: A framework for curriculum and instruction.* Alexandria, VA: Association for Supervision and Curriculum Development.

Maykut, P., & Morehouse, R. (1994). *Beginning qualitative research. A philosophic and practical guide.* London: Falmer Press.

Mayring, P. (1995). *Qualitative inhaltsanalyse: Grundfragen und techniken* [Qualitative content analysis: Basic questions and methods] (5th ed.). Weinheim, Germany: Deutscher Studienverlag.

Mayring, P. (1999). *Einführung in die qualitative sozialforschung* [Introduction to qualitative social research] (4th ed.). Weinheim, Germany: Beltz.

McDonough, J., & McDonough, S. (1997). *Research methods for language teachers.* London: Arnold.

McKernan, J. (1988). Teacher as researcher: Paradigm and praxis. *Contemporary Education, 59*(3), 154–158.

McNamara, M., & Deane, D. (1995). Self-assessment activities: Toward autonomy in language learning. *TESOL Journal, 5*(1), 17–21.

McRae, J. (1991). *Literature with a small 'l'.* Basingstoke, England: MEP/Macmillan.

McRae, J. (1992). *Wordsplay.* London: Macmillan.

McRae, J., & Boardman, R. (1984). *Reading between the lines.* Cambridge, England: Cambridge University Press.

Meyer, M. (1997, September). The GREENing of learning: Using the eighth multiple intelligence. *Educational Leadership, 55*(1), 32–34.

Miles, M. B., & Huberman, A. M. (1994). *Qualitative data analysis.* Thousand Oaks, CA: Sage.

Millrood, R. (2004). The role of NLP in teachers' classroom discourse. *ELT Journal, 58,* 28–37.

Mjagkij, N., & Cantu, D. A. (1999). "The public be damned!" A thematic and multiple intelligences approach to teaching the gilded age. *OAH Magazine of History, 13,* 56–60.

Morita, N. (2004). Negotiating participation and identity in second language academic communities. *TESOL Quarterly, 38,* 573–603.

Müller-Hartmann, A. (1999). Die integration der neuen medien in den schulischen fremdsprachenunterricht: Interkulturelles lernen und die folgen in e-mail-projekten [The integration of the new media in the foreign language classroom: Intercultural learning and the consequences in e-mail projects]. *Fremdsprachen Lehren und Lernen 28,* 58–79.

Müller-Hartmann, A. (2000). The role of tasks in promoting intercultural learning in electronic learning networks. *Language Learning & Technology, 4*(2), 129–147.

Nakahama, Y., Tyler, A., & van Lier, L. (2001). Negotiation of meaning in conversation and information gap activities: A comparative discourse analysis. *TESOL Quarterly, 35,* 377–405.

Nakatani, Y. (2002). *Improving oral proficiency through strategy training.* Unpublished doctoral dissertation, University of Birmingham, England.

Nespor, J. (1987). The role of beliefs in the practice of teaching. *Journal of Curriculum Studies, 19,* 317–328.

Nicholson-Nelson, K. (1998). *Developing students' multiple intelligences.* New York: Scholastic.

Norman, S. (Ed.). (2003). *Transforming learning: Introducing SEAL approaches.* London: Saffire Press.

Nunan, D. (1988). *The learner-centered curriculum.* Cambridge, England: Cambridge University Press.

Nunan, D. (1989). *Designing tasks for the communicative classroom.* New York: Cambridge University Press.

Nunan, D. (1992). *Research methods in language learning.* Cambridge, England: Cambridge University Press.

O'Dowd, R. (2003). Understanding the "other side": Intercultural learning in a Spanish-English e-mail exchange. *Language Learning & Technology, 7*(2), 118–144.

Oliver, R., & Mackey, A. (2003). Interactional context and feedback in child ESL classrooms. *Modern Language Journal, 87,* 519–533.

O'Malley, J. M., & Chamot, A. U. (1990). *Learner strategies in second language acquisition.* Cambridge, England: Cambridge University Press.

O'Malley, J. M., & Valdez Pierce, A. (1996). *Authentic assessment for English language learners.* Reading, MA: Addison-Wesley.

Osguthorpe, R. T., & Graham, C. R. (2003). Blended learning environments: Definitions and directions. *Quarterly Review of Distance Education, 4,* 227–233.

Oxford, R. L. (1990). *Language learning strategies: What every teacher should know.* New York: Newbury House.

Oxford, R. L. (1997). Cooperative learning; collaborative learning; and interaction:

Three communicative strands in the language classroom. *Modern Language Journal, 81*, 443–456.

Oxford, R. L., & Ehrman, M. (1993). Second language research on individual differences. *Annual Review of Applied Linguistics, 13*, 188–205.

Pathak, S. (2000). *Race research for the future: Ethnicity in education, training, and the labour market* (DfES Research Report RTP01). Nottingham, England: DfES.

Patrick, B. (2001, April). Students matter: Student retention: Who stays and who leaves. *University of Glasgow Newsletter, 227*. Retrieved May 17, 2006, from www.gla.ac.uk:443/newsdesk/newsletter/227/html/news15.html

Pérez Basanta, C. (1994). Interview with John McRae. *GRETA, 2*(2), 35–41.

Prabhu, N. S. (1987). *Second language pedagogy.* Oxford, England: Oxford University Press.

Rautenhaus, H. (1995). Können e-mail texte zur förderung von fremdsprachlicher kompetenz und kulturverständnis beitragen? [Can e-mail texts contribute to the promotion of foreign language competence and intercultural competence?] In L. Bredella (Ed.), *Verstehen und verständigung durch sprachenlernen?: Dokumentation des 15. Kongresses für fremdsprachendidaktik, veranstaltet von der Deutschen Gesellschaft für Fremdsprachenforschung (DGFF), Giessen, 4-6. Oktober 1993* (pp. 311–320). Bochum, Germany: Brockmeyer.

Reid, J. (1997). *Understanding learning styles in the second language classroom.* Englewood Cliffs, NJ: Prentice Hall/Regents.

Richards, J. C. (1990). The dilemma of teacher education in second language teaching. In J. C. Richards & D. Nunan (Eds.), *Second language teacher education* (pp. 15–32). New York: Cambridge University Press.

Richards, J. C., & Nunan, D. (Eds.). (1990). *Second language teacher education.* New York: Cambridge University Press.

Richards, J. C., & Rodgers, T. S. (2001). *Approaches and methods in language teaching* (2nd ed.). Cambridge, England: Cambridge University Press.

Richardson, V. (1994). Conducting research on practice. *Educational Researcher, 23*(5), 5–10.

Riel, M. (2000). Learning circles make global connections. In R. Donath & I. Volkmer (Eds.), *Das transatlantische klassenzimmer* (2nd ed., pp. 136–163). Hamburg, Germany: Körber-Stiftung.

Riley, A. (1991). *English for law.* Harlow, England: Longman.

Roberts, J. (1998). *Language teacher education.* London: Arnold.

Sachs, J. (2003). *The activist teaching profession.* Buckingham, England: Open University Press.

Samuda, V. (2001). Guiding relationships between form and meaning during task performance: The role of the teacher. In M. Bygate, P. Skehan, & M. Swain (Eds.), *Researching pedagogic tasks* (pp. 119–140). Hemel Hempstead, England: Pearson.

Savignon, S. (1991). Communicative language teaching: State of the art. *TESOL Quarterly, 25*, 261–277.

Scharle, A., & Szabó, A. (2000). *Learner autonomy: A guide to developing learner responsibility.* Cambridge, England: Cambridge University Press.

Schmitt, N. (2001). *Vocabulary in language teaching*. Cambridge, England: Cambridge University Press.

Schommer, M. (1990). Effects of beliefs about the nature of knowledge on comprehension. *Journal of Educational Psychology, 82,* 498–504.

Schön, D. (1983). *The reflective practitioner: How professionals think in action*. New York: Basic Books.

Seliger, H., & Shohamy, E. (1989). *Second language research methods*. Oxford, England: Oxford University Press.

Sigel, I. E. (1985). A conceptual analysis of beliefs. In I. E. Sigel (Ed.), *Parental belief systems: The psychological consequences for children* (pp. 345–371). Hillsdale, NJ: Lawrence Erlbaum.

Sinclair, J., & Coulthard, M. (1975). *Towards an analysis of discourse*. London: Oxford University Press.

Skehan, P. (1989). *Individual differences in second language learning*. London: Arnold.

Skehan, P. (1998). *A cognitive approach to language learning*. Oxford, England: Oxford University Press.

Slavin, R. (1985). *Learning to cooperate, cooperating to learn*. New York: Plenum Press.

Smagorinsky, P. (1995). Multiple intelligences in the English class: An overview. *English Journal, 84,* 19–26.

Smith, D. M., & Kolb, D. A. (1986). *The user's guide for the learner style inventory: A manual for teachers and trainers*. Boston: McBer.

Sommers, E. (1993, March/April). *Learner-centered, not teacher-abandoned: Peer response groups that work*. Paper presented at the 44th Annual Meeting of the Conference on College Composition and Communication, San Diego, CA.

Soo Hoo, S. (1993). Students as partners in research and restructuring schools. *Educational Forum, 57,* 386–393.

Spiro, R. J., Feltovich, P. J., Jackobson, M. J., & Coulson, R. L. (1992). Cognitive flexibility, constructivism, and hypertext: Random access instruction for advanced knowledge acquisition of ill-structured domains. In T. M. Duffy & D. H. Jonassen (Eds.), *Constructivism and the technology of instruction: A conversation* (pp. 57–75). Hillsdale, NJ: Lawrence Erlbaum.

Spolsky, B. (1989). *Conditions for second language learning*. Oxford, England: Oxford University Press.

Spratt, M. (1994). *English for the teacher*. Cambridge, England: Cambridge University Press.

Stapleton, P. (2003). Assessing the quality and bias of Web-based sources: Implications for academic writing. *Journal of English for Academic Purposes, 2,* 229–245.

Stenhouse, L. (1975). *An introduction to curriculum research and development*. London: Heinemann.

Stenhouse, L. (1985). *Research as a basis for teaching*. London: Heinemann.

Stern, H. H. (1992). *Issues and options in language teaching*. Oxford, England: Oxford University Press.

Strickland, D. (1988). The teacher as researcher: Towards the extended professional. *Language Arts, 65, 754–764.*

Swales, J. M. (2002). Integrated and fragmented worlds: EAP materials and corpus linguistics. In J. Flowerdew (Ed.), *Academic discourse* (pp. 1–25). London: Pearson Education.

Tarone, E., & Yule, G. (1989). *Focus on the language learner: Approaches to identifying and meeting the needs of second language learners.* Oxford, England: Oxford University Press.

Teele, S. (1996). Redesigning the educational system to enable all students to succeed. *NASSP Bulletin, 80*(583), 65–75.

Teele, S. (2000). *Rainbows of intelligence: Exploring how students learn.* Thousand Oaks, CA: Corwin Press.

Tieg, B., Bailey, C. R., Arllen, N. L., & Gable, R. A. (1993). *Effects of collaborative vs. noncollaborative structures on the learning and adjustment of elementary schools students.* Norfolk, VA: Old Dominion University. (ERIC Document Reproduction Service No. ED 360 798)

Townshend, K. (1997). *E-mail: Using electronic communications in foreign language teaching.* London: Centre for Information on Language Teaching and Research.

Trim, J. (2001, September). The work of the Council of Europe in the field of modern languages, 1957–2001. Paper presented at a symposium to mark the European Day of Languages, European Centre for Modern Languages, Graz.

van Lier, L. (1996). *Interaction in the language classroom.* London: Longman.

Vogt, K. (2001). E-mail-projekte am berufskolleg—Not worth a light? [E-mail projects at vocational schools: Not worth a light?] *Fremdsprachenunterricht, 45,* 416–422.

Wallace, M. (1998). *Action research for language teachers.* Cambridge, England: Cambridge University Press.

Walsh, S. (2003). *Enhancing interactional competence through reflective practice.* Paper presented at the IATEFL TTEd SIG Conference, Exploring Interaction in Teacher Education, University of East London.

Wang, M. (1983). Development and consequences of students' sense of personal control. In J. M. Levine & M. C. Wang (Eds.), *Teacher and student perceptions: Implications for learning* (pp. 213–247). Hillsdale, NJ: Lawrence Erlbaum.

Ware, P. (2005). "Missed" communication in online communication: Tensions in a German-American telecollaboration. *Language Learning & Technology, 9*(2), 64–89.

Warschauer, M. (1996). *Telecollaboration in foreign language learning.* Honolulu: University of Hawaii Press.

Weber, E. (1996). Creative communities in high school: An interactive learning and teaching approach. *NASSP Bulletin, 80*(583), 76–86.

Weiner, B. (1986). *An attributional theory of motivation and emotion.* New York: Springer-Verlag.

Wenger, E. (1998). Communities of practice: Learning as a social system. *Systems Thinker, 9*(5). Retrieved May 28, 2005, from http://www.co-i-l.com/coil /knowledge-garden/cop/lss.shtml

White, C. (1999). Expectations and emergent beliefs of self-instructed language learners. *System, 27,* 443–457.

Widdowson, H. (1975). *Stylistics and the teaching of literature.* Essex, England: Longman.

Williams, M., & Burden, R. (1999). Students' developing conceptions of themselves as language learners. *Modern Language Journal, 83,* 193–201.

Willis, J. (1996). *A framework for task-based learning.* Harlow, England: Pearson.

Winn-Smith, B. (2001, January). Classroom language. *English Teaching Professional, 18,* 12–14.

Wolf, L. B. (1996). Student autonomy, student responsibility: Some elements involved. *Aspectos didácticos del Inglés, 5,* 51–84.

Woodward, T. (1991). *Models and metaphors in language teacher training.* Cambridge, England: Cambridge University Press.

Wragg, E. C. (1994). *An introduction to classroom observation.* London: Routledge.

Wright, T. (1987). *Roles of teachers and learners.* Oxford, England: Oxford University Press.

Wylie, R. (1979). *The self concept.* Lincoln: University of Nebraska Press.

Yoshida, K. (1996). Intercultural communication as interpersonal communication. In G. van Troyer, S. Cornwell, & H. Morikawa (Eds.), *On JALT 95: Curriculum and evaluation. Proceedings of the JALT 1995 International Conference on Language Teaching/Learning* (pp. 95–103). Tokyo: Japan Association for Language Teaching.

Zeuli, J. S. (1994). How do teachers understand research when they read it? *Teaching and Teacher Education, 10,* 39–55.

Index

Page numbers followed by an *f* or *t* indicate figures and tables.

A

Also Available From TESOL

Bilingual Education
Donna Christian and Fred Genesee, Editors

Bridge to the Classroom: ESL Cases for Teacher Exploration
Joy Egbert and Gina Mikel Petrie

CALL Essentials
Joy Egbert

Communities of Supportive Professionals
Tim Murphey and Kazuyoshi Sato, Editors

Content-Based Instruction in Primary and Secondary School Settings
Dorit Kaufman and JoAnn Crandall, Editors

ESOL Tests and Testing
Stephen Stoynoff and Carol A. Chapelle

Gender and English Language Learners
Bonny Norton and Aneta Pavlenko, Editors

Language Teacher Research in Asia
Thomas S. C. Farrell, Editor

Literature in Language Teaching and Learning
Amos Paran, Editor

More Than a Native Speaker: An Introduction to Teaching English Abroad
revised edition
Don Snow

Perspectives on Community College ESL Series
Craig Machado, Series Editor
Volume 1: Pedagogy, Programs, Curricula, and Assessment
Marilynn Spaventa, Editor
Volume 2: Students, Mission, and Advocacy
Amy Blumenthal, Editor

PreK–12 English Language Proficiency Standards
Teachers of English to Speakers of Other Languages, Inc.

Planning and Teaching Creatively within a
Required Curriculum for School-Age Learners
Penny McKay, Editor

Professional Development of International Teaching Assistants
Dorit Kaufman and Barbara Brownworth, Editors

Teaching English as a Foreign Language in Primary School
Mary Lou McCloskey, Janet Orr, and Marlene Dolitsky, Editors

Teaching English From a Global Perspective
Anne Burns, Editor

Technology-Enhanced Learning Environments
Elizabeth Hanson-Smith, Editor

For more information, contact
Teachers of English to Speakers of Other Languages, Inc.
700 South Washington Street, Suite 200
Alexandria, Virginia 22314 USA
Toll Free: 888-547-3369   Fax on Demand: 800-329-4469
Publications Order Line: 888-891-0041
or 301-638-4427 or 4428
9 am to 5 pm, EST

ORDER ONLINE at www.tesol.org/

T E S O L